Gairfish

Edited by W.N. Herbert & Richard Price

The

McAVANTGARDE

Edwin Morgan, Frank Kuppner, Tom Leonard, Kathleen Jamie

The unpublished MacDiarmid

First published 1992 by *Gairfish*

Gairfish is edited by W. N. Herbert and Richard Price. Forbes Browne is Business Editor. Submissions of essays and poetry should be sent to: Forbes Browne, *Gairfish*, 34 Gillies Place, Broughty Ferry, Dundee, Scotland. As well as typescripts, work submitted on five-and-a-quarter inch disk, but always accompanied by a neatly typed typescript, will also be considered. Future topics planned include: 'MacDiarmid: A Centenary Celebration', and 'Women and Scotland'.

Gairfish is dedicated to publishing creative work in all the languages of Scotland. It is also committed to the radical reappraisal of Scottish culture without adherence to any faction, political or otherwise. However, *Gairfish* does not consider its rubric to be limited to Scottish writers or affairs: its aim is the greatest plurality possible stemming from a Scottish base.

Gairfish is still £3.50 per issue and £6.00 for two. If you wish to subscribe in advance of publication it will only cost £3.00 per issue. Cheques should be made payable to *Gairfish*. Larger donations and assistance are acknowledged in each issue.

Friends of Gairfish: Frank McAdams, I. Neil, J. B. Pick, D. J. Taylor. Special thanks to Donny O'Rourke.

The letter from C. M. Grieve (Hugh MacDiarmid) to William Jeffrey appears by courtesy of Maeve Kinloch and the permission of the copyright holder Michael Grieve, who also very kindly gave *Gairfish* permission to reproduce the previously unpublished MacDiarmid poem.

Typeset in Scotland by Black Ace Editorial, Ellemford, Duns, TD11 3SG.

We are delighted to acknowledge subsidy from the Scottish Arts Council towards the publication of this volume.

ISBN 0 9515419 43 (pbk) £3.50

Contents

Scotia Nova: *Edwin Morgan* 4

Editorial: McAvant-Garde, *W. N. Herbert* 5

A Door, a Gingerbread, and Death to Strathclyde Region,
Richard Price 13

Poems by: *Maoilios Cambeul, Peter Daniels,
Margaret Elphinstone, Michael Glendening* 18

Essay: Thoughts about a Scottish Literary Avant-Garde,
Robert Crawford 26

Poems by: *James Aitchison* and *Graham Fulton* 32

Gustav Mahler, a Five-act Drama: *Frank Kuppner* 42

A Night at the Pictures: *Tom Leonard* 46

Poem: *Peter McCarey* 48

Essays: Scotland – Made from Girders?, *Richard Price* 51

The Nomadist Manifesto, *Kenneth White* 61

The Autonomous Region, *Kathleen Jamie* 69

Poems by: *Bob Cobbing, Elizabeth James, Keith Jebb,
Tom McGrath, Hugh MacMillan,* 74

Documents: A Letter to William Jeffrey, *Hugh MacDiarmid* 87

All that is good, *Hugh MacDiarmid* 89

Features: Sidney Goodsir Smith, *John Manson* 90

The Scottish Avant-Garde in the 1960's, *D. M. Black* 96

The Apology of a Dictionary-Trawler, *David Kinloch* 98

Poems by: *David Kinloch, Duncan McGibbon, John Dory,
Vittoria Vaughan* 101

Translations:
Walloon Poetry, Introduced by: *Yann Lovelock* 113
Brecht, translated by *J. M. Andrews* 120

Essays: Modern Poetry in Scots, *Kathleen McPhilemy* 121

The Tum-ti-tum Epithet, *Peter McCarey* 131

Tradition and the New Alliance, *Alan Riach* 135

Grasping a Thistle: Scotland and the Visual Arts,
George Wyllie 146

Poems by: *W. S. Milne, Robert Alan Jamieson,*
and *Tom Hubbard* 153

Virtual Scotland: The Word Tax, *Pseudorca* 156

EDWIN MORGAN

Scotia Nova
(with apologies to Robert Burns)

O wha my maglev-buits will buy,
O wha will prent my jaggy cry;
Wha will kick me when I lie,
The avant-gaird the daddie o't.

O wha will own he's cracked the faut,
O wha will dye his mince wi maut,
O wha will bell the gird and ca't,
The cuttin-edge the daddie o't.

When I growk an cheek the chair,
Wha will grin an guide me there,
Gie me Joab's Balances an mair,
The avant-gaird the daddie o't.

Wha will back me i'the fast lane;
Wha will sneck the foostie fane;
Wha will bigg me ower again,
The cuttin-edge the daddie o't.

W. N. HERBERT

Post-Neo-Futurism,
Or, The Progress Of The Pugilistic Pseud

When I could last afford to stay in Venice, nearly three years ago, my wife and I were trundling along our usual narrow route from the Calle dei Vinanti to the Rialto when we stumbled across a subtle diversion. The statue of a more than portly young woman had been dragged into the middle of a tiny crossroads with a sign indicating the whereabouts of the sculptor's studio. This sudden change in a rather touristy section might not have made much impact had the statue not been dancing with such vulgar abandon. We followed the sign.

The sculptor, Matteo Lo Greco, was in the midst of a cramped saraband of large women dancing, stretching, reclining, caressing each other and themselves; extraordinary bronzes that seemed buoyant, the earth mother as barrage balloon. I was reminded of the Scottish painter Gwen Hardie, but the overwhelming impression was that someone had done something rude with a Giacometti and a bicycle pump. Anyway, all this is irrelevant as we could scarcely afford his catalogue, let alone his smallest statue. The point of this anecdote is that I asked for and got an English translation of his group's manifesto.

This, the 'MANIFESTO OF THE UNAUTHENTIC' was an especial delight to me on a number of grounds. Not only was the translation awful, but its very existence established that a very European phenomenon, the self-styled *avant garde*, was alive and well. Having always delighted in the thoroughness of the Italian Futurists, who declared war on pasta, I wanted this small scrap of oddness to take home to Britain (this was pre-Reeves,

THE AIRFISH DEFIES G

you understand):

> An image, painted, sculpted, or described, can assume one hundred dimensions and ad [sic] many layers, if its creator, free of any preconditioning, is capable of formulating and realizing them.

This was the essence of Edwin Morgan's title *Themes on a Variation*. It is the multiverse as visioned by Terry Pratchett, in which an alien wizard, momentarily manifesting on a midatlantic jet, naturally metamorphoses into a David Lodgeian academic. It is the Trattoria Filanti in Montecerignone from which Umberto Eco was rushed to hospital on New Year's Eve with a suspected heart attack, in what looks like a suicide attack by a vengeful *lasagne al forno*. We hung the manifesto in the toilet and waited for a reaction from guests.

Nothing, of course. Who in Britain would dare comment, in case, you know, it wasn't a *joke*, or perhaps it was? What artist in Britain, lugging his or her statuary into the middle of a pedestrian thoroughfare, would dare to be the member of an actual *group*? What writer would consider stating their actual opinions and intentions in anything as incriminating as a *manifesto*? There are places, like 'Pseud's Corner', for such people. In Britain, and particularly in that wretched aesthetic outhouse known as 'North Britain' or 'Frail Caledonia', what the UNAUTHENTICS term 'preconditioning' manifests itself as an urgent need to apologise in advance for the social discomfort caused by culture.

The persistent and obstinate neglect of those figures in twentieth-century British literature who did address themselves to a modernist concept of the *avant-garde*, such as Wyndham Lewis and Hugh MacDiarmid, is reflected in the current marginalisation of troubling Scots like James Kelman and Alasdair Gray, or in the preferment of Irish writers over Scots like Morgan or Kenneth White. These poets' work awkwardly relates back to MacDiarmid instead of lacing in to an assimilated tradition like that of Yeats. Barbara Harlow, in *Resistance Literature*, refers us to other instances of this stratagem of 'divide and rule':

> Masao Miyoshi, in his reading of twentieth century Japanese novels, 'Against the Native Grain,' warned against the dangers of either 'domestication' or 'neutralization' in the study in the West of non-western literary works. Whereas the danger of 'domestication' is that it renders all too familiar, and thus subjudicates through assimilation, the challenge posed by the unfamiliar, the alternative of 'neutralization,' which categorically rejects and isolates the unfamiliar as finally irrlevant, is no less a threat.

A common misconception of the prominent place granted to Irish poetry within 'English' literature is that this is justified by the urgency of a poetic driven by the 'Troubles'. Without underestimating for a moment the important role played by middle-class guilt in all cultural decisions, the point should perhaps be made that the traditional prosody of a great deal of modern Irish writing permits the English to domesticate it without too much violence to their own post-Movement definition of verse. The polite bafflement with which recent manifestations of experimentalism in the work of Paul Muldoon and Seamus Heaney have been greeted would tend to support this thesis.

A Scottish parallel to the tactic of polarising authors into limiting definitions has surely been at work in assessing the two most significant writers of Scotland's first *avant-garde* movement, the Scottish Renaissance, Neil Gunn and Hugh MacDiarmid. With only a few exceptions, Gunn's centenary appears to have passed in an orgy of postcard views designed to present him as tame Highland novelist, rather than a radical rethinker of this lachrymose genre. In MacDiarmid's case we have yet to see how much or little will be done with the forthcoming centenary to redress the gaping holes in Scotland's analysis of its most significant Modernist poet.

One area of MacDiarmid's achievement which is relevant to this argument concerns what Umberto Eco termed 'semiotic guerilla warfare.' This was the creation of Synthetic Scots, the Modernist language par excellence, in which cultural meaning could be defined, it seemed, as emphatically as in a Poundian ideogram or, as Curtius said of Olson, a Mayan glyph. The issue did not prove this simple, as Tom Leonard established in the sixties by foregrounding a politicised Scots orthography, continuing what Eco called 'a *tactic* of decoding where the message as expression does not change but the addressee discovers his *freedom of decoding.*'

Modern Scots, which combines synthetic and demotic elements, has been forcefully 'neutralized', to use Miyoshi's term, by Scotland's elder stuttersmen as clinging to an outmoded fashion, a failed experiment. Scots Language poets like Robert Crawford and David Kinloch are in fact approaching the question from a radically new angle, one which has affinities with the tactics of new Scottish poets writing in English like Peter McCarey and Alan Riach. All these writers are re-exploring Modernist tenets of composition for non-Modernist effects; as Riach says:

> You can see
> MacDiarmid's language
> advancing
> in directions of production
> which were probably never guessed
> at

Essentially, then, writers in Scots are examining the validity of different kinds of discourse. Can a 'folk' phrase still have a rural emphasis if employed by an urban poet? If a word from the sixteenth century is placed next to one from the twentieth, which term dominates? The effect resembles on the one hand Boccione's theory of *paroles in libertas* (words-in-freedom), and on the other the more contemporary experiments of the American

L=A=N=G=U=A=G=E poets. In fact Lyn Hejinian's comment on their techniques, 'where once one sought a vocabulary for ideas, now one seeks ideas for vocabularies' is forcefully reminiscent of MacDiarmid's adaptation of Mallarmé to his own purposes:

> Because of a profound interest in the actual structure of language, like Mallarmé's, like Mallarmé I have always believed in the possibility of 'une poesie qui fut comme deduite de l'ensemble des proprietés et des caracteres du langage' – the act of poetry being the reverse of what it is usually thought to be; not an idea gradually shaping itself in words, but deriving entirely from words – and it was in fact [. . .] in this way that I wrote all the best of my Scots poems [. . .]

It is also precisely in this way that writers like Crawford and Kinloch are recontextualizing Scots. Yet, like the work of the Language poets, which offers among other things a critique of the bankrupt vocabularies of capitalism, this is not merely an aestheticism. Such experimentation, because of Scotland's historic record of linguistic subjugation, must always carry a political overtone. These are necessary stages in the creation of an independent speech, the S=C=O=T=S of a *nazione in liberta*.

The results would suggest Standard English is merely a variation from which we may discover new themes, whole 'new found land's in which even dead words respire, as happened on December 20th 1682, when the French scientist Seguin, in order to test the theory that living toads are found inside treetrunks, opened a block of plaster of Paris inside which 20 toads had been trapped 12 years previously. Four of them were still alive. In Scotland we are more fortunate, in that only the tongues of the upper classes were encased in plaster of London. The rest of us, though afflicted by education, have been producing both themes and variations for some time.

In the 1960s Scotland's second *avant-garde* movement entered the international scene on quasi-independent terms. That is, it did not consider the English mainstream for its model, but looked, as contributors to this issue suggest, to America, France, and in the case of the Concretists, to Brazil. But in doing so, as D. M. Black points out, it was in fact aligning itself with the beleaguered English *avant-garde*. While the various Paladin publications and anthologies have begun the process of re-establishing Tom Raworth, Lee Harwood and others, that aspect of the Scottish wing which concerned itself with the Scottish radical tradition has not yet been seen as a concerted movement. It is one of the aims of this magazine to gather up these loosened threads.

Poets like Edwin Morgan and Kenneth White, who have been extending the principles behind MacDiarmid's late work to apply to their own separate concerns, do not deserve to be dismissed witht he familiar tag of post-modernism. It would be fairer to say that White, in his commitment to larger works and open form, and Morgan, in his concern to keep admitting the vocabularies of modern technology into his verse, as well as in his championing of science fiction as a Scottish poetic tradition, are effectively reModernists, working to extend the premises of Modernism, rather than merely liberalize them. In this they can be said to have provided an example for the younger poets I have been discussing.

Throughout this editorial I, like the coiners of the phrase '*avant-garde*', have been flirting with militaristic metaphors despite my own pacifism. Yet neither my own country nor the example of eastern Europe would suggest there is any positive result from or need for armed republicanism. I would like to return, then, to the 'UNAUTHENTICS', with their less aggressive (and less grammatical) premise of art as a limitless sequence of parallel universes. One of the great joys of manifestoing seems to be the freedom to create one's own gobbledegook instead of having to put up with the gobbledegook of government and advertising. I have had a go with the 'Scots L=A=N=G=U=A=G=E' and the 'reModernists', now let's listen to the professionals (one last military reference there):

> The new dimension represented by the 'UNAUTHENTIC' is a psycho-scientific dimension, more mnemonic at mass level, more a displacement of relation (metaphysical + induced motion) atropic medianic penetration, more the metamorphosis of an apparition, more the successive realization of many creations, more the hypothesizing genetic expression of one or more heretofore nonexistent realities; but which one day will come into being just because they were enunciated.

My imagination wanders off somewhere around 'atropic medianic penetration', which sounds like a New Age can-opening technique, but I can appreciate that last naive statement of faith in the autonomous power of the word. God had a similar theory, I believe, or was that Chomsky? Anyway the point is there's little use in being afraid of the *avant-garde*; those who take refuge in ridicule always seem to end up as the ones being ridiculed by posterity. It's a well-known fact in *really* outré circles that the rebel angels did not in fact rebel, they were thrown out for laughing when the Deity mentioned He was thinking of creating the three-toed sloth. And the expulsion from Eden had nothing to do with Eve; God just got a little bit testy when Adam called His latest pride and joy a 'guppy'.

This issue of *Gairfish* heralds Hugh MacDiarmid's centenary year. The next will be an examination of his achievement from a variety of new perspectives, with the particular intention of lacing him in to the twentieth-century tradition as evinced by other Scottish writers, rather than idolizing him as a unique phenomenon. The refusal to put our major writers in their proper historical context has in the past led to the partial denial that such a coherent context exists, let alone links up with any other to form a literature.

The issue after that will be a women's issue, for which contributions are now invited. The guest editor will be announced in the MacDiarmid issue. *Gairfish* is now distributed widely throughout Scotland and England, but we are still reliant on our subscribers to maintain our standards and regularity of production. It still costs only £3 for one and £6 for two issues in advance of publication, and that includes postage. If the next two issues interest you, then you can help us by ordering them now. Remember:

> With the 'MANIFESTO OF 2000' we 'UNAUTHENTICS' want to reawaken the torpid, deluded, tired, lying in the dust of flat conformism the consciousnesses [sic], and incite them to get up, to walk, to run, to fly with us towards new words of knowledge and of the science of the future.

RICHARD PRICE

A Door, a Gingerbread, and Death to Strathclyde Regional Council

1

I was recently in New York's Whitney Museum of Modern Art, a gallery which, though well laid out and spacious, is small enough to present a sense of coherence. This also means it can alternate its paintings often enough to make even a fairly regular visitor see something new from its icebergish collections. While I was in one room a group of a dozen or so eight- or nine-year olds came in with their enthusiastic teacher. She stopped them in front of a Willem de Kooning and put her hand across the title. The children were rather free with their opinions, all of which were dismissive of what to them was just paint and colour pasted across a canvas in a rather insulting meaningless way. They also wanted to read the title first, but the teacher said that too many people home in on the caption of a painting before they do anything else – if they do anything else. Painting in most cases, she said, is not about two or three pieces of language tacked on to the wall beside a frame.

The restless children wanted to move on to something more recognisable, but the teacher said that they had first to take a good look at the painting and try and say something about it. What did it make them think of? One boy said, rather cheekily I thought, it made him think the guy had spilt some paint. The children laughed. The teacher said that maybe you're right – it does remind you of paint itself, rather than some of the other paintings they had seen which were more about the subjects themselves – still life, portraits, or whatever. So maybe this painter was doing something a little different, but the important thing was it was not anything we couldn't understand.

With her hand still on the caption, the teacher then asked them again to say what it made them think about. A girl said part of it looked like a kind of door. The teacher asked her to save what she had said for later. Then another girl said maybe there was some sunshine there, and also a river on one particular part of the canvas. The teacher said that was very interesting. Asking one of the boys who had originally been so derisive to read it out to the rest, she took her hand away from the caption. His eyes widened and he laughed. 'Door to River,' he said.

2

Two years before my mother died, she gave me a painting. She'd not been pleased with it: the appearance of distortion offended her draughtswoman's eye. A still life, huge dark foliage swirled in a hefty black jug, blooms fussed in darknesses, leaf and flower embroidered a whirlpool. She said it was too modern and wouldn't waste my birthday with it, but I was impressed. One Railcard visit the untitled had got framed – I took it home with a gingerbread.

Finished with oils for the time being she straightened and opened a buckled box of water colours, the first time she'd 'washed', she said, since 1941. She'd finished school at fourteen, enjoyed I think two years at an art college and then left for the 'real world', to parental relief. A husband and four sons intervened until she took up brushes again in her fifties. After practice, her watercolours seemed exact, translucent, light. Her flowers were almost prissy with accuracy; polite china replaced the junkish jug of her oil painting. Not my cup of tea I almost said.

She left me her brushes, pared pencils, although I can't draw.

I remember her enjoying some of my poems, but mostly enjoying the fact of them – not reading too many to keep from disappointment. But as if I was an art critic and an artist she'd show me her pictures and ask my opinion.

3

Ian Hamilton Finlay is one of our most interesting avant-garde artists. One of his successes has been the conquest of ordinary objects with art: postcards, neon lights, drains, a garden, a board game. He has even supplied errata for classical texts. The thought of Ovid being subject to a consistent printer's error is not so daft as it appears: just what do we respond to when we read or view any work of art if not some element of distortion between creation and presentation? There is also that lovely playfulness Finlay has. I'm reminded of a correction slip added to one of Alasdair Gray's novels: 'This erratum has been inserted by mistake.'

Perhaps my favourite Finlay object is his blue badge which has the inscription (originally from a sun-dial):

```
EVEN
-ING
WILL
COME
THEY
WILL
SEW
THE
BLUE
SAIL
```

When I have worn this badge a number of people have independently assumed that this was part of a prayer. There is a religious resonance, as if the 'they' of the poem might be some divine spirits who actually sew the blue evening in order to sail it at night. It also suggests to me the shared night-work of a fishing community (Finlay's work often features fishing boats), and in this I suppose there is that feeling of fraternity that one is meant to feel when one is being religious. Certainly it has been a very effective way of introducing friends to Finlay's work, not least because it gives no indication of the brutality that is at the tight heart of much of his work.

Signs declaring 'Death to Strathclyde Region' seem funny enough to dismiss, but artistic eulogies on Second World War German tanks, machine guns, and Nazi decals are a little harder to take. His political philosophy, however, is not as facile as that suggested by the apparent fascism of his little boys' games. For example, his work of the last ten years celebrates the revolutionariness of the French Jacobin, Saint-Just, hardly a fascist icon, and his long-standing feud against Strathclyde takes seriously the trope of the artist being pitted against a small-minded but big-muscled bureaucracy. Such a stereotypical situation, though discussed often enough by artists in tones of resignation and martyrdom, and squawked over by funders, is not usually thought through by either group. Finlay makes you reconsider the conflict as if it was of the utmost importance, which it is.

In a sense, he re-launches death into art. This he does with the honed sentence. Like William Blake's proverbs from Hell they shock with their exploding excess, they excite, and they make you feel *that radical*. The 'clean-ness' of his forthright statements are almost conceptual slabs in themselves: he seems to successfully enjoy the relationship between the purity of typography, sculpture, and the deft and challenging phrase. Stephen Baum, via Friedrich von Schlegel, has called this 'a species of wit which, because of its purity, precision and symmetry, we would like to name architectonic wit.' A re-expression of that emphasis on the architectural absolutism of Finlay is to say that his work intensely *avoids distortion* both on the sculptural and literary plane, as other avant-garde artists in fact enjoy or re-use it. Indeed, the degree to which an artist successfully connects with and re-configures the distortion around and within him or her may actually define the degree to which that artist brings new ideas into being. The severe and the mis-shapen are carrying us.

MAOILIOS CAIMBEUL

Brìgh

An solas a' sireadh
na sùla
mus robh na sùilean ann
a' siubhal a' chearcaill agus lionsa.

Ioma-dhathte –
bogha-frois an aoibhneis
bogha-frois a' bhròin

camera a' gabhail dhealbhan.

Solas a' siubhal
an t-sùil a' feitheamh
glaist' anns an t-solas.

Tonnan a' briseadh
ann an galacsaidhean gun chrìoch
fuaim a' feitheamh na cluaise.

Brìgh ro bhith.

Essence

Light looking
for the eye
before eyes were
seeking iris and lens.

Multi-coloured
rainbow of gladness
of sorrow

a camera taking pictures.

Light seeking
the eye waiting
locked in light.

Waves breaking
in endless galaxies
sound waiting
the ear essence
before existence.

A' Chraobh Beithe

Chan e dath an airgid
uile a th'air a' chraoibh beithe;
tha dath na meirg oirre cuideachd
 – agus dath na fala.
Na gasan òga dorcha
mar gu robh iad ag radha
slàn leis an talamh.
Airgead dath na h-inbhe
cruinn le sanas de phinc.
Nas àirde geugan
a' fàs dearg-dhonn a-rithist
agus gan cuairteachadh a' breabadaich
nèamh air choreigin
na duilleagan còire.

The Birch

The birch is not all silver
rust also
the colour of blood.
The saplings dark
as if saying
goodbye earth.
Then mature silver
round with a hint of pink.
Higher branches
reddish brown again
and all around rustling
some heaven or other
kindly leaves.

PETER DANIELS

Excesses of the Prior of Inchcolm
(Deposed from office, 1224)

A monk is illuminating
aspects of the deadlier sins.
The Prior is much in his mind.
The blue snake twined
round the capital of Pride
follows his long smooth shape.
Something of his in the smirk
of the Scarlet Whore.

The Prior does not inspect the work.
He strides freely, he is not afraid
of the hellfires they resentfully
score down for him. Along this road
he will elevate self and soul: to see
his priority shining out beyond
the stony shape of the cloistered island.

A Video of my Father

At ease among statisticians, he settles into his chair
to trace back his subject for the archives.
His developing concepts arise, like The Advancing Wave
in a Spatial Birth Process. My nonsense-mind is
daydreaming probabilities, how I am where I am.

Telling of southward-moving mathematicals, 'We
Scots . . . ' he remarks; taking me aback, though he keeps on
a few Scots consonants. Always he is fondest of Leeds:
his first job, the Wool Research Board, drawing out
meanings from thousands of snapped-off ends of yarn.

London-Jewish baby, carried back north to where
Grandmother's herring boat came in. Families don't
add up. Look for some balancing factors: at the piano,
grasping the precision of Chopin; learning from a neighbour
the reconstruction of a watch, counterpoint of ratios.

At home, intepreting Grandmother's cabbage soup, her
Yiddish-Russian, her mental arithmetic. Bar-Mitzvah:
God's rules to measure the arbitrary lives, the walk
from synagogue to tenement door. Desire for the true
parameters, from the simple Standard Deviation, to

The Maximum of a Random Walk. But where I have walked
is not his Edinburgh: this window, years after his mother
nailed it up. From her time, I have one early memory: the lace,
the teacups, Arthur's Seat, railings at Portobello. No Scot,
no Jew, it's not mine: except the remainder recurring.

MARGARET ELPHINSTONE

Cocoa de Mer

Cocoanut of the sea
Washed up on Indian shores
From submarine forests,
A legend without a ground,
Till Europeans found strange trees
In the Seychelles,
Forced their secrets,
Then stripped the magic seeds
To the shores of extinction.

I hold in my hands
The largest seed in the world,
Cocoa de Mer, smooth, heavy,
Rounded, like the statuettes
Of fertile women, washed up
From the lost past.

The seed is catalogued
Under palm species
(endangered),
On a library shelf,
A far cry from the forests
Of the past,
While the magic islands
Are stripped of cover
And sink back into the sea.

MICHAEL GLENDENING

Hieroglyph

In a brightly painted wooden coffin someone
Has been wrapped in blackened linen.
Her unbandaged foot is black with resin.

A serpent, text, and a procession
Have been painted on the dark coffin,
And on her body linen. Over the cased specimen

A wooden, originally golden, winged thing flies.
As her soul travelled from one world to the next
Did it stop to read the text?

Or, trapped within a decaying coffin,
Did her unconscious dim, did it blacken?

ROBERT CRAWFORD

Thoughts About A Scottish Literary Avant-garde

Belatedness is a curse of Scottish culture. Readers soon grow accustomed to opening an anthology or a magazine of 'now' Scottish poetry only to find it filled with a considerable proportion of work that could have been produced several decades ago. It might be argued that this is no bad thing, that it demonstrates the independence of Scottish culture from the modish and ephemeral. Yet the maintaining of such a stance is ultimately an arrogant insularity which results in Scotland being excluded from intellectual developments in Europe and beyond. It encourages a Scotland that is more at home with the dead than the living, a 'here's tae us' culture whose peers are damn few and aw deid.

It would be an act of showy self-pity to complain that the problem of belatedness was in any way unique to Scotland. Belatedness is a universal concern and is bound up with our natural love of cliché. Words that are tried and tested, words that have shaped us (but which we have not shaped) are always the standard medium of communication, the preferred, familiar, stuff of journalism, official documents and ordinary conversation. As far as verse is concerned, the bad poem is bad not because it sounds uniquely awful, but because it sounds just like a lot of other poems, because it sounds exhaustedly familiar. The good poem learns from the past; the bad poem repeats it like a cliché. Part of the poet's maturing involves an avoidance of repetition – a learning process which demands wide reading. You can steal, you can reincarnate, you can even quote in a new context, but simple repetition is ossification, death. Each poet to write authentically has to tune into and build upon the language of his or her age, the locutions, the tones, the speed. To do otherwise is inauthentic. The language of Wordsworth's age was not that of Dryden's.

Being true to the language of an age is not necessarily the same as conforming to the poetic taste of an age. That is why the *Lyrical Ballads* had to develop a preface, and why Eliot felt he had to inveigh against the popular 'annual scourge of the Georgian anthology.' In a sense Wordsworth and Coleridge (like the young Carlyle of *Sartor Resartus)* were clearly avant-garde artists, yet we seldom if ever speak of them as such. The term avant-garde tends to be used only of artists within the last hundred years, and has come to be associated in Anglophone literature particularly with Modernism, and most particularly of all with the High Modernism of Eliot, Pound, Joyce, Wyndham Lewis, and their cronies. If there was a quintessential avant-garde magazine, for instance, then surely that magazine was *Blast*.

'We are still learning to be James Joyce's contemporaries' begins Ellmann's life of Joyce. There can be little doubt not only that Joyce was in some senses 'ahead of his time', but also that he managed to capture that time – its rhythms, its secrets, its growing awareness of psychology, its available kinds of language and behaviour. Joyce was a product of his age, but not of the predominant literary taste of that age. That made him, like Eliot and Pound, an avant-garde artist.

In a forthcoming book, *Devolving English Literature*, I have argued that MacDiarmid should be seen in his rightful place both as one of the major Modernists, and as part of a Scottish tradition which contributed significantly to the development of Modernism. Considering such a view alerts us to the problems of belatedness and the Scottish literary avant-garde, MacDiarmid is not just writing alongside Eliot and Joyce, he is reacting to them. He is making a tremendous effort to absorb the new European ideas of his era – reading both *Ulysses* and *The Waste Land* in Montrose in 1922 – and to galvanise the rest of Scotland into making contact with them. But some might argue that MacDiarmid's great efforts only bring him to the rear of the avant-garde. *A Drunk Man* follows *The Waste Land* and *Ulysses*. It would be hard to think of any ways in which MacDiarmid anticipated those works. And if one feels that about MacDiarmid, then what of his Scottish contemporaries? The anthologies of quaintly titled *Northern Numbers* read like a Scottish Georgian anthology, or perhaps something less interesting. Whatever their merits, few of MacDiarmid's colleagues in the Scottish Renaissance could be considered avant-garde figures in the international arena. Even today the work of Edwin Morgan, often thought of in Scotland as ultra-modern, draws a good deal of its formal 'modernity' from the Russian poetry of sixty or more years ago. Morgan has also undertaken a salutary but at times forlorn effort to alert Scots to contemporary artistic developments elsewhere (such as $L = A = N = G = U = A = G = E$ poetry), but the reaction which still greets some of his formally 'experimental' work is surely a function of Scottish belatedness.

So widespread is this belatedness that it has made for the intense loneliness of avant-garde figures working within Scotland. The avant-garde artist usually works in spite of, rather than through or alongside the cultural *status quo*. Institutions such as universities, established magazines, grant-giving bodies and writers' groups, may often frustrate rather than further his or her aims.

The best such an artist can hope for in the immediate short-term is a small coterie of sympathetic fellows, like the group gathered round *Blast*. Avant-garde art is usually thought of as metropolitan – the huge, mixed population of the metropolis providing enough members for the coterie, or (if the art fails) the clique.

In Scotland, however, avant-garde work has tended to be produced in isolation. *Sartor Resartus* was composed at Craigenputtock; much of MacDiarmid's late poetry was written on Whalsay; Ian Hamilton Finlay works in his garden at Stonypath; *A Drunk Man* was produced not in Edinburgh but in Montrose. Perhaps the closest we come to a metropolitan avant-garde is in the contemporary group of Glasgow writers which includes Alasdair Gray, Edwin Morgan, Liz Lochhead, Tom Leonard, and James Kelman. Yet these writers, though they know one another, are notably uneasy about being considered as any sort of formal group. Moreover, there is observable in the work of several of them a concern with being isolated from the community in which they live and work, even as they seek links with that community. This is exemplified best in the work of Tom Leonard when he pictures the artist standing in the dole queue, unable to make real contact with the working class, or when he pictures the literature professor Edwin Morgan as 'said to exist . . . in an unobtrusive block of flats off Great Western Road', but being in fact 'Cultural attaché to the legendary city of Morganiana', a fantasy kingdom rather than an actual location. A detached and isolated figure in the midst of the crowded city and its much-used libraries, Morgan's younger contemporary, the poet and novelist Frank Kuppner, seems to exemplify the loneliness of the Scottish avant-garde artist who is either geographically marginalised from the centres of population or else, in the midst of such centres, has to exist in an awkward cultural isolation.

No doubt a considerable degree of loneliness is the fate of any avant-garde. To escape the belatedness of his own culture, and its naive political pressures, Joyce left Ireland for continental Europe, knowing what Joseph Brodsky has articulated for the present generation, that ultimately the best and only duty of an artist is to write well. We Scots might learn from the work of such exiles as Joyce, Brodsky, and Stanislaw Baranczak how best to deal with some of our cultural and political pressures when we write. A striking number of avant-garde Scottish writers this century have chosen to remain within Scotland, but their stay may have constituted a lonely internal exile. In conventional parlance the avant-garde refers to a body of artists. Often in Scotland, though, our avant-garde seems to be a single individual.

I am writing in an effort to win sympathy and support for the position of the isolated avant-garde artist in Scotland, which is not quite the same as rattling the can for our cultural organizations. These can easily contribute to the climate of belatedness through refusing to engage with contemporary ideas outside Scotland. Coming to grips with such ideas may not mean accepting them, but it is definitely not the same thing as jamming them out. Nae postructuralism in Scotlit! Nae French feminism! Nae paying of attention to contemporary American poetry since the New York School! It is not unusual to meet Scottish poetry enthusiasts who know very little at all about contemporary poetry written outside Scotland. Such eyes-on-the-buits Little Scotlandism is exactly the opposite of the attitude which MacDiarmid or Morgan have attempted to encourage, and is a betrayal of our cultural traditions. An avant-garde figure such as Ian Hamilton Finlay is an effective counter to such a betrayal. In the face of a general anti-intellectualism and insular as well as belated attitudes in Scottish writing, Finlay is at once Scottish and international. With or without collaborators, he simply goes his own way, as courageously as did MacDiarmid. He is our avant-garde, alone.

To compare Finlay and MacDiarmid may seem ludicrous. For though MacDiarmid's letters show that he gave much encouragement to the young Finlay, they also demonstrate his bitter opposition to Finlay's mature work in concrete poetry when (ironically) Finlay and Morgan were Scottish elements at the forefront of an international avant-garde. By the 1960s and 1970s many of MacDiarmid's views had become markedly reactionary. Though he had produced in the Thirties a body of work with which we have yet fully to come to terms, and which has fuelled later writers such as Morgan, MacDiarmid wrote no new significant verse after 1939. By the heyday of concrete poetry he was both out of touch and out of sympathy with new developments. His published correspondence with Tom Scott reveals that he was prepared to use literary blackmail in order to prevent Finlay's work being included in a new *Oxford Book of Scottish Verse*. MacDiarmid told Scott that he would allow none of his own poetry to be included if any of Finlay's verse was in the anthology. In this regard at least, MacDiarmid had passed from being avant-garde to being narrow-mindedly and viciously reactionary.

So far in this article, I have used the term 'avant-garde' as if it were either a value-free label, or even a term of praise. For many it is neither. This quasi-military term, so much associated with the art of more than fifty years ago, has come to seem dated. Often the avant-garde's isolation has gone hand in hand with an apparent or actual elitism. We might sympathise with this when it is a product of courageous loneliness, of being surrounded by a belated taste; yet not when it broadcasts for Mussolini's radio, or advocates a species of Scottish fascism, or condemns to oblivion the English or the Jews. Not only in the work of Larkin and Movement writers, but also in the attitudes of such Scottish poets as MacCaig and Dunn one detects a hostility towards the notion of an avant-garde. This hostility accompanies a wish for a genuinely popular and accessible democratic poetry closer perhaps to the tradition of Burns than to the often elitist work of MacDiarmid. Yet MacCaig's poetry and Dunn's criticism also exhibit an enormous admiration for some of MacDiarmid's achievement. This is a gesture of awe and generosity, but it is also a limiting gesture. If it became an orthodoxy, we would be left too soon with the tame, domestic MacDiarmid of comfy Scot Lit courses, whose later work would be exiled to the domain of Unpoetry.

It is this very 'poetry of fact' which may be most quintessentially Scottish, and most daring in MacDiarmid's output, coming out of the factual eclecticism of the Scottish Enlightenment encyclopedists, out of Scott, Carlyle, and Davidson, and which has been so important not only to Morgan but also to younger writers. We should guard against MacDiarmid's Stalinism. We should react suspiciously to his *dicta*, but it would be wrong to settle for any easy attempt at domestication which ignored some of his most adventurous work. The result would be that he ceased to pose for his readers great, exciting aesthetic problems and became instead another dishtowel Burns, a flagwavers' literary gonk.

Scotland has such a small population that the audience for 'advanced' writing is bound to be minute, and the audience for 'advanced' poetry even smaller. The sort of infrastructure – an adventurous poetry-reading audience, committed distribution networks – is lacking to such a degree that it may well be impossible for us to sustain solely out of our own resources any significant avant-garde artist. One need only think of how much help MacDiarmid and more recent Scottish figures received from outwith Scotland, not least from the USA. To some extent this need for the Scottish avant-garde artist to rely on support from outside Scotland may be a good thing. It will ensure that he or she keeps in touch with contemporary international developments, a must if mere repetition is to be avoided. Yet if a stage were reached where such a Scottish artist can find *no* local audience in his or her own lifetime, then the situation would have become terminal. Scotland would have become a mere backwater of perpetual belatedness. It would be healthier at present to see more contemporary first-rate work from outside Scotland appearing alongside new Scottish work in Scottish publications, just as one would wish to see more contemporary Scottish work available in translation abroad. Cross-fertilisation is a two-way process, vital not just to an avant-garde but to anyone who takes writing seriously.

We may not wish to strive consciously for a literary avant-garde, if by that we mean to pursue to the exclusion of all else the pursuit of experimental fiction, drama, and verse. It is hard, though, to imagine a Scotland whose culture was entirely dominated by experimental writing! – so perhaps some pressure for greater sympathy to be given to the predicament of a Scottish literary avant-garde is no bad thing. Such an avant-garde needs flexible financing; it is not likely to attract major corporate sponsorship. No avant-garde can be created by financial decree. It may not wish to call itself an avant-garde, or even a number of avant-gardes of one. It may wish to strive for closer identification with the Scottish people, or it may not. If it helps free us from cliché it will at any rate further our democracy. It may wish to get rid of the elitism fostered by the label 'avant-garde' – which could help it admit more women. It is likely to be helped by a publishing house such as Polygon, if Polygon survives, but it may establish its own, stranger or non-native channels. It could result in spectacular success or spectacular failures. It could go unnoticed in Scotland for years. If we take the attitude that some sort of Scottish avant-garde, under whatever name, is undesirable, or too intellectual, or should be studiously ignored, then we shall be shooting ourselves in the foot and in higher places also. For ultimately what a literary avant-garde offers is an escape from the rule of verbal cliché, political cliché, and social cliché. It offers danger and sometimes potential destruction. We need 'traditional' artists to warn us of its extremes and to avert its threats. Without it, though, there will be no changes except those which are decreed exclusively from outside Scotland. We should be left eventually in a perpetual kailyard – of pastiche Black Mountain School or repetitions of the early Heaney, or (in 2020) of re-run John Ashbery – a kailyard of belatedness.

The best art has no sell-by date, but is sometimes a slowly acquired taste. Inferior art has a sell-by date, but we frequently choose to ignore it. When was the last time you checked the Scottish produce on your shelves? If the old, abrasive, elitist, phallocentric notion of an avant-garde is beginning to go stale, it's about time we looked for a new one.

JAMES AITCHISON

from **Neurological Rounds**

Mr William Sloane   Admitted 29 August   Broca's Aphasia

'Lesions in Broca's area. He had a fall.'

Where did she say? It was in Ashton Street.
I was doing the even numbers in Ashton Street.

'Thank you, Sister. Good morning, Mr Sloane.
What can you tell me about yourself this morning?'

'Pain . . . tuh . . . pain . . . '
Long ago, but I've seen these two before.
'Pain . . . tuh . . . pain . . . tuh . . . ray . . . '
I was never much of a talker but this is mince.

'Pain? An X-ray to locate the pain?'

'I think Mr Sloane's telling us
he's a painter, a painter and decorator.'
'Yes. Aphasia. Certainly. Yes. And Broca's? Yes.
Now I should like to hear some more of him.'

'Do you know why you're here, Mr Sloane?
Can you tell Mr Makjian why you're here?'

Does she mean why I'm *here*? *This* hospital?
Meaning mental. But it's just the words.
I thought the Vicky or the Western G.,
being the nearest to Ashton Street.
Thank God it's just a phase.
'Loss . . . loss . . . wors . . . '
Surely to God they know it's just the words.

Can't get them from my brain to my mouth.
'Loss . . . fuh . . . loss . . . fuh . . . wors . . . '
But not mad. 'Not . . . not . . . mmm . . . '
Shut it, Sloaney. Find another word.
She asked you if you knew why you were here.
'Fall . . . fall . . . fall . . . '

'Splendid, Mr Sloane. You had a fall.
What can you remember about your fall?'

'Effing . . . evering . . . effering . . . '
The sun, the sun on my back, and the smell
of primer covering up the smell of scorch
where I'd burned off and sanded the day before.
'Pain . . . ti . . . pain . . . ti . . . '
Ing, for God's sake, Sloaney. Ing as in ing.
'Pain . . . ti . . . painti . . . winnow . . . fame . . . '
The brush going to and fro, the easy flow
of primer whitening the window frame.
And the funny feeling, the lovely feeling you feel
when you stand at the top of the ladder, the sun on your back,
and watch yourself watching the brush going to and fro.
'Jam . . . uh . . . jam . . . winnow . . . frame . . . '
A heave at the frame. Another heave –
'Fall . . . een . . . tide . . . uh . . . slide . . . fall . . .
evenside . . . uh . . . Ashn . . . Ashton Street . . . '

'You were painting window frames on the even side,
the even number side, of Ashton Street
and then you fell. Splendid, Mr Sloane.
Splendid. You remember everything.'

Everything? One second? Two seconds?
Falling a long, long time.

'Sister, how soon can therapy begin?
Tomorrow. Yes. Tomorrow, Mr Sloane.'

But there's therapy and therapy.
There's physio and then there's –
Don't say it, Sloaney. You couldn't, anyway.
Try physio. 'Physi . . . phys . . . uh . . . physi . . . o . . . '

'It may persist, the fizzing in your head.
The lesions in Broca's area, that is . . .
the poly synaptic reflex arc. The left
hemisphere . . . the inferior frontal lobe.
Your left ear, Mr Sloane, not the ear itself
but . . . how would you say it, Sister?'

'Just above your left ear, Mr Sloane.
Imagine a little area inside your head
just above and in front of your left ear.
Your fall has damaged the little bit of your brain
that helps you to speak, and read and write.'

Signwriting as well?
I was never much of a talker, a reader or writer.
But the signwriting:
black Roman capitals of Andrew Strang,
Rods & Guns since 1899;
the Gothic gold of Antique Maps and Prints;
the slim italics of computafile.

'Mr Makjian thinks speech therapy might help
in your case, but there's no guarantee.
We'll see what Mrs Scott says tomorrow morning.'

Speech therapy. Thank God for that.
Did she say that before? Speech therapy?

'Mr Makjian can't make promises
because we can't repair your synapses,
the little junction boxes in your brain,
transformers and transducers.
But you'll still be able to do everything else.'

I couldn't do as much as that before.

'Your job, for instance. You'll still be able to paint.
And gardening. Are you a gardener?
No? There's lots of other things, Mr Sloane:
walking, swimming, or even a little jogging;
driving, travelling, sightseeing;
darts or draughts or dominoes or bowls.'

Oh aye? I wish I'd fallen off years ago.

'Radio, television, photography.
You could even try your hand at something new:
angling, cooking music, home-made wine.
Yes. Why don't you try your hand at something new?
After all, you're a different person now.'

Different? I thought she said it's just a phase.
'Not . . . a . . . phase . . . a . . . phase . . . ?'

'Yes, Mr Sloane. Aphasia. Loss of speech.
Some reading and writing also will be lost,
but all the properties of your right hemisphere,
that is, your visuospatial skills . . . I mean –
sketching. You will do sketching, Mr Sloane,
and all the splendid things that Sister said.'

Sketching. Aye. I like the sound of that.
Sketching and therapy, speech therapy.
And this feeling, this daft feeling again,
top-of-the-ladder feeling, the sun on my back

now that I know what's happening.
'Ha . . . Hap . . . happe . . . ' Try glad, for God's sake, Sloaney.
'Glad . . . glad . . . tuh . . . hap . . . hap . . . happe . . . '

'You are glad and happy, Mr Sloane?
Splendid. Tomorrow therapy begins.
I shall return on Friday, Mr Sloane.
We shall have another splendid chat.'

* * *

'He speaks as if he were inventing speech.
The network damaged, without synapses
for grammar or syntax, is a new network,
each word uttered as if for the first time
and with the artlessness of first attempts.
The simplest form, the simplest sound of the word:
nouns, but no plural nouns;
verbs without a past or future tense;
not "I have fallen" or "I shall fall"
but the stammering, unconditional simplicity –
"Fall. Fall. Fall."
No. No. I speak like a barbarian.
Mr Sloane, he has sensation still
and memory enough to make a world.'

Mr R S Crosier   Admitted 15 July   Wernicke's Aphasia

'Good morning, Mr Crosier. How are you?
What can you tell Mr Makjian this morning?'

'Good morning to you. I am morning.
Sir, I say you are no starry paladin
but a reprician – reprician – reprician –
But I diverse, and I apologise.

I say you are patrublican –
partrub – patrib – patrublican.
In otherliness you are repatrian.'

'You are very generous, Mr Crosier.
Others deserve your kindness more than I.
Sister Murray here, and Mrs Scott.'

'I understand. Firenze – Firenze luscinia
and all immately larchicals, without whom
I have no sleeping now or waking then.
But you, young sir – Although I am old
and speak my age I am as morning
in the good morning of repatrians.'

'Splendid, Mr Crosier. Your speech improves.
And you co-operate with Mrs Scott?'

'In principling but not in genesis –
suffix – genesis – suffix – No, sir. No.
You are the refutable suffix of your suffix.
The confutable of your suffix.
In otherliness the herisable nymbus.'

'You mean my name? My nationality?'

'No, no, young sir. I do apologise.
The principling of statelessness –
I hear my voice diverse again.'

'Your voice is clear, Mr Crosier.'

'My voice is clear, sir, and I say to you,
you are of the eagle stockists and patrublicans.
Repatrian as I once wished to be;
as you are now, sir, and shall be.
I must not halt your pilgrimage

but I say these things while I am morning,
while there are chalices – chalices –
while there are galaxies inside your head.
Not Avalon, sir. Never Avalon.
In my head once, and now in yours, young sir.'

'I am most grateful, Mr Crosier.
Republic or kingdom? It is enough to know
we recognise the same infinity.
On Friday you will tell me more
for I have much to learn.'

'Just rest now, Mr Crosier. I'll come for you
at half-past ten and take you to Mrs Scott.'

* * *

'One of the other sisters on the course
said it was just like someone speaking in tongues.
You weren't meant to hear her but you did
and for a moment you looked ill with rage.
"Divinity?" you said. "Divinely inspired?
Possessed by a holy spirit? A holy ghost?"
And then your anger turned to sarcasm:
"Or do you think religious ecstasy
is caused by lesions in the frontal lobe?"
Tap-tap-tapping with your fingertips
behind your left ear; rapid little thuds.
"A holy ghost with Wernicke's aphasia?"
Somebody laughed. You wavered, and then smiled
and went on lecturing. At the end you said
the intervention of the holy ghost
had made that lecture memorable.'

'I meant my anger. I apologise.'

'No. I remember some of the arithmetic:
ten billion neurons and ten billion more
synapses – Mr Crosier's galaxies? –
and half a million words and variants,
and personal accent and vocabulary –
you clicked a slide: *Lexicon, Idiolect* –
that make each person's speech unique.
You got us thoroughly confused and then you said
the figures proved we must not hope to find
meaning in the Wernicke aphasic's speech.
"You may hear a greater frequency
of abstract nouns," you said, "or passive verbs,
but what you hear is the patient's patholect,
sound and meaning irreparably split
in a non-language we cannot translate
because we have no code." Another slide:
Phonology, Semantics, Patholect.
We were hopelessly confused. 'Listen,' you said,
'listen to tone and quality of voice,
the tempo, volume, rhythm and the pitch.
You must tell your patients this," you said;
"your patients and your nurses and yourselves:
Aphasia means that language has been lost
and the lost words may never again be found,
but the patients still have power to think and feel.
Aphasia means a small part of the brain
is lost; the patients have not lost their minds."'

'I said these things. Yes. You remember well.
And you remember there was something more?'

'Yes. "When the patients take our word for it . . . "'

GRAHAM FULTON

One hundred and fifteen in sixty seconds

Outside SCOTTISH POWER
a man is trying to break
his one arm press up
world record.

The crowd is hushed.
His blood
pumps. His T-shirt
is white. His face
wears a smile as
he nears his goal.

He was run over by a bus
and once considered killing himself
but took up body-building instead.
'Things looked black'

according to the DJ
who keeps an eye on
his chunky watch that
tells the time in Singapore, who wears
a silky designer suit, who keeps
a copy of Patsy Cline's CRAZY
in a shopping trolley and
his turntables at
the ready.

'Whutsgawnon?'
says an old man with
a 'Plants of the Bible' carrier bag.

A yankeee flag shellsuited lad
lollops past and rockets a gob.
People push in to pay the bills.
Their faces wear smiles as they reach
the counter
next to the hoovers and
radio clocks.

Ten seconds left.
He's going to be close.

The yodelling contest starts
in three minutes.
Good sports
have been asked to HAVE
A BASH.

FRANK KUPPNER

Gustav Mahler
A Five-Act Drama

ACT ONE

(Chatter; 1901; sparkling lights; November; scents; almost incomparably well-chosen furniture; some pretty central street in Vienna; a reassuring meal has just ended, or is just ending; Klimt; in person; witty discussion; amicable discussion; mordant discussion; several neurotics present; the precise words are unrecorded.)

ALMA MAHLER: Vorsinflutliche Gebräuche! But I simply do not understand how the public has allowed this to happen!

MAHLER: You are an ignorant possessor of juvenile ovaries. Only someone young, some damsel who habitually faints into her ice-cream, could ask such a dumb question. Someone who knows nothing about cowardice and compromise. Whereas I know all there is to know about such subjects.

ALMA MAHLER: This simply cannot be him. (Faints.)

ZUCKERKANDL: I have never seen him so at ease in society before.

KLIMT: Tiglath Pileser!

(A meal just like real grown-ups give.)

ACT TWO

(First day of the year. A bedroom. Not next door.)

MAHLER: Verzweiflung! Am I Johannes Brahms? Why? 32 seconds more and I'd have managed to do it! I feel as useless as a Tele-mann flute concerto.

ALMA MAHLER: Don't be too er harsh with yourself, Gustav. It's not important. We're not married yet. It might well have ruined our lives anyway. Please stop doing that.

MAHLER: Can I be already past it? It was never like this in Hamburg. Or Budapest. Or Kassel. Or Preussisch-Elau. Or Pyritz. Or Dorpat. Or Prenzlau. Or Neu Ruppin. Or Pasewalk. Or –

ALMA SCHINDLER: I had no idea you had spent so much time in the North, Herr Mahler.

MAHLER: Oh, horizontal cleavageperson! Fantastische Landschaften! Has it all descended to this? I step down from the train and realise I am old.

ALMA MAHLER: Don't weep for shame, Gus. You are only forty and this bed would depress anybody.

MAHLER: I have never got anything completely right in my whole life. Whereas, even your hair – (Weeps, but not for shame.)

ALMA MAHLER: I just can't help thinking at times it was the mental anguish that did it.

ACT THREE

(Several dozen hours later. The same place, presumably. Needless
to
say, they have been away and come back. Quite possibly one
of them has been drinking. Perhaps both. The Emperor is not
asleep.)

ALMA: Heloise! 1100 to 1164! Joy beyond all joy! Atzenbrugger
Dances! Oh, the mere proles will never be able to do this!

MAHLER: Tristan und Isolde! It passes the time I suppose. I
contain the entire Austro-Hungarian Empire! Only now do I truly
understand what the phrase 'in and out' means. Surely I have been
a disappointment to my mother.

ALMA: Only then did I realize what a master of orchestration
he was.

MAHLER: Lift your leg and stop flashing those lights.

ALMA: Are we totally in control? Will you write something about
this? Do we have History exactly where we want it? It needn't be
an entire symphony. My dead father made bad mistakes too, but
he became a successful painter. Eventually.

(The unwanted mystery of creation will shortly occur.)

ACT FOUR

(Six years later, plus. His first child, conceived just after the pre-
vious act, has just died of diphtheria. The grounds of Schönbrunn
Palace. A bench. 1907, I think. Arthur Schnitzler, born 1862,
from a distance catches sight of Mahler seated on a bench, and
wonders how anyone can survive such events. Fate will see to

it that he more or less finds out for himself. Various childhood crises. Uniquely she was allowed to disturb him whenever she wanted to. Clearly, something is in his mind. But if so, what? Our mindlessness produces such beauty. And other forms of mindlessness scrub it out. Stop passing by! Please! Another dead leaf blowing down the path.)

MAHLER:

ACT FIVE

(Perhaps a minute or so is left. 18 May 1911. Late at night. Stormy night. But many good and bad burgers sleeping anyway. Others hurry through the streets, not safe in warm beds. I suppose the storm must subside long before it reaches the place where my German-speaking grandparents have not quite yet conceived their fifth, their last, and – from the present point of view – their most necessary child. Well, take your time. Let us give him twenty more seconds. Now five more, before his final recorded utterance. Is it utterly reliable? Oh, most beautiful of escapes! Schubert!)

MAHLER: Mozart!

(Dies, smiling with intense love at his wife; who is having an affair with an architecture student. So it continues.)

TOM LEONARD

A Night at the Pictures
[after Duhamel] – for Sonya

Some time ago my wife Sonya and myself went to the Glasgow Film Theatre, formerly the Cosmo. We went to see a French film called *Jean de Florette*, which had received same good reviews. Unfortunately between our house and the cinema, my wife and myself had a row. I cannot remember what it was about, or any of the details; but as we entered the cinema she delivered a particularly wounding remark, in a quiet voice. I was not going to sit having a night-out as if nothing had happened, but to storm out would have been histrionic. As the film began I therefore found that I was staring at a position on the ceiling somewhere north-west, five to eleven, of the screen itself.

The position of my head was such that a person who did not have a sight of my eyes would have assumed that I was watching the film. I did not want to disturb anyone else in the cinema by making a public issue of my estrangement from the communal event. Gradually I began to 'take in' where I was – without moving my position other than the occasional quasi-relaxational shift that would divert potential awareness in others of an unnatural rigidity in one of the group.

The dialogue that filled the theatre seemed a little harsh and loud, as if it needed some adjustment to the volume and the treble. Also the words were in French, which did not help me, as I only understand it at a simple level, spoken slowly. There were long periods without dialogue, the sound of what was perhaps a cow, of people breathing. Feet on floors, utensils, sounds that indicated a scene indoors. Voices evidently shouting from a distance meant that the action had moved once more outside. The most dramatic point was when the cinema was suddenly filled with the sound of a thunderstorm, while a man shouted at the top of his voice, then started weeping. All the while I kept my eyes averted from the screen. A couple of times my wife asked me if I was all right. I replied that I was.

Away from the screen, the quality of light that the screen threw on the walls and ceiling was surprisingly mixed, jumpy, changing all the time; I could see the varied light on the crowns of people near the front, the varying darkness at the small of their backs. Inevitably – I was in an end seat in the balcony – I could see angled shoes at the aisle's edge opposite, the usual light at the carpet shining on a man's sock at the ankle. But it was the silence that really struck me: the silence of the people around me, above all the silence of the building that was not this talking wall at which I couldn't look. The door with its sign EXIT – saying nothing. The building revealed itself as a wall of silence, literally, between the screen and the world. This in the red light that shone faintly on my wife and myself, noticeable in the darker moments, from one of the pinlights above us.

Then it was over, and we were out. I felt I had maybe gone beyond a mark, broken a primitive taboo between friends. But to have called it the breaking of a primitive taboo would maybe have been to load it with a significance it did not deserve. After all, it had just been a huff. When asked how I had enjoyed the film, I had to admit that I had not seen any of it. But by the time we reached home, I had been told most of the story, and the row was already almost forgotten.

Months later the sequel to *Jean de Florette* – a film called *Manon des Sources* – came to the same cinema. We decided about eight o'clock one evening to go, and got to the cinema just after the film began at half past. We were sitting in the forward region, in the last row of what is called the front section of the theatre. We were in a good mood. No question of a huff tonight.

After a short while my wife remarked that the opening seemed to be the same as the last one. I thought that perhaps this was a runthrough, a kind of reminder of what had taken place in Part One. Or else it was employing the device of beginning and ending the film with the same images, to make some artistic point – like Polanski's *Repulsion*, or the sound of the carcrash in Losey's *Accident*. But this was not the case. It was simply that for the benefit of those who had not seen the film before, the cinema was showing *Jean de Florette* today, Wednesday. The sequel, *Manon des Sources* would be shown on Thursday, Friday and Saturday. We had made a mistake.

But my wife had enjoyed the film on its first showing, and she generously agreed that we should just sit there again. So the sounds that had formed for me an incomprehensible abstract were now united with their visible images. I was a member of the audience with my companion, and saw nothing of what I had seen so stealthily before.

PETER McCAREY

In the Metaforest
(for M.C.)

The story's more familiar in reverse:
Your suitor lolloped in from a neighbouring tale;
He snuck into your bed and swept you off in his sedan,
electric windows closing with a snick.
You got no sleep at nights, no rest in days,
yet something in you slept like folded cream,
Rose-o'-the-Winds.
You were trying to tell the fruiterer
(she of the grass-green silks and velvets)
that her apples weren't fit for stewing, and she said:
'a houseful of helpless weans you've got
they'll not do a hand's turn for you
stuck in that poky wee flat all day
with the door on the chain cause you're
feart of the neighbours. Aye, I know
they buy you flowers, they get them here.'

One day you left a note:
'There's seven dinners in the oven.'
Your hair turned black,
you slimmed into the clothes you used to wear.
You met a stranger in the woods, quite kind
at first, but then veiled threats,
and something about a knife. You got away
unscathed, but how come here you are
in another suburban flat?
For the first time you remember

to take a long look at yourself.
The mirror tells you, with regrets,
your newly acquired stepdaughter
is a lot more cute than you. This makes your day
black, or maybe green, but is it middle age? maturity?
It doesn't really matter. Look in the glass:
It says you look just fine, ever after all.

The story's for you, but it isn't yours. Now stop.
Rewind to the tangled forest. Stop.
O see ye not yon narrow road,
so thick beset with thorns and briars?
That is the path of righteousness.
Proceed one hundred yards, and stop.
There's a fork in the road, and a legend etched in stone:
Go this way and lose your life
go that way and lose your mind
Rose-o'-the-Winds. Observe the wych elm
above your head: a bough extends
above your head, and from that bough
a pale hand dangles, nay gesticulates (maybe
you had noticed it already). Take it
in both your hands, I'll pull you up:
it's a cosy place – but what do we do now?

Public Opinion

Well kids, now that we're changing reels
and Roy has commenced his death-defying,
laser-guided leap toward
the scalp of the redskin riding bareback
up the gulch below, I'd like to ask you a question:
should he (a) twist aside and grab that branch
growing from the canyon wall,
avoiding pain to himself and the brave
who is, after all, obeying orders, or
(b) follow through, unseat the Iroquois,
seize the tomahawk wrist with his left
and neutralize with the right? Hands up
if you think that (b)'s the answer.
Hmm, that's pretty interesting. What's that son?
What do you mean you've got reservations
about the conduct of this survey?

'85% of the British people support the war in the Gulf'
– *Moskovskie Novosti*, 17 February 1991

Targetted cohorts and randomized clusters
of folk who subscribe to the phone and the vote are
collected and sorted, recycled and sold.
Mustered at dawn, at stops and stations,
the khaki electorate creases and smooths
its brow, its mucoid camouflage tissues,
its tabloid columns and quality rags.
In infra-red light districts
midnight splatter movies roll.

RICHARD PRICE

Scotland: made from girders?

Scotland: made from girders? The title of this essay is a twisted form of an advertisement, for Irn Bru of course, because it is the advertisement form that seems to me to be the most concentrated kind of image. And it is with images, images of Scotland, that we are interested today. The advert achieves with the sketchiest of symbols a richness of identifications and sympathies seldom found elsewhere, and because it necessarily makes assumptions about its reception it is true to say I think that the advert not only reflects society it tries to interpret it. However, before I get on to our other national drink, or even the 'original' one, I want to talk about how Scotland in particular is advertised.

Living and working for much of my time in London, I have the dubious privilege of seeing how Scotland is being portrayed to what must be a massive cosmopolitan market. Scotland is marketed in one series of posters, with alternative versions in German, French, and Italian, as a 'different holiday every day.' The meaning of this slogan, as the accompanying photographs show, is that not only can you fish for salmon, look at moorland, and buy Caithness glass, you can enjoy urban clubland, too. You see, Scotland's so varied it has not only countryside but cities.

This surprising and complex aspect has been taken up in another of the Tourist Board's catch-phrases: 'Come to Scotland and enjoy a culture shock.' The supporting photo for this one pictures a curling pond on which are foregrounded a ballet dancer's feet. The shock is not so much the different types of cultural activity as such, it is that there should be capital C culture in Scotland *at all*. I am conscious that I may be speaking with the superior advantage of the typical London Scot, whom James Naughtie in a recent *Listener* article has called 'more patronising than patronised', but I would argue that there is more than a chip on the shoulder behind this sensitivity.

It is perfectly understandable, of course, for the tourist board to project their product as a country of Enjoyment, with variety in its scenery and its entertainments. Clearly there is a need to educate and inform, and the Tourist Board may be doing what any tourist agency can only do: provide a superficial dazzle that will generate interest and of course cash. But cash for who?

What really grates about the Tourist Board's publicity is the disjunction between the neatly edited Holiday Country and Scotland itself. 'Scotland' in a meaningful political sense, that is where Scots themselves have control of their own lives and resources, has not existed for hundreds of years. Even when there was a Scottish Parliament it was, like the current Westminster Parliament, hardly a model for democracy. From even before 1707 Scotland has been a kind of Hardy's Wessex: a semi-country whose attraction to outsiders, and perhaps to insiders, too, is that it *once* existed. The idea that it should exist again is taken to be Nostalgic Escapism, when in fact keeping Scotland servilely in this sub-state of being plays on exactly the same notion of cultural reminiscing. When some want to go beyond Nostalgia – to bring Scotland into a position where Scots can make their own decisions, this is perversely regarded as romantic idealism. Indeed even some on the left would rather have Scotland under a London monarchy than consider a Scottish republic. The republic, it seems, goes against working class principles.

The Tourist Board adverts are nevertheless good examples of an important change in the way Scotland has been presented to outsiders in the last ten years. Up until the eighties, the Highlands were, ironically, Scotland's selling point: for hundreds of years, a containable, malleable wilderness. An important aspect was the element of 'otherness' – their scenic scale, and their 'foreign' natives who have 'alternative' values (luckily, one is reassured, these values include hospitality). With all these in mind, the attainable remoteness of the Highlands has meant that they have become a psychological sop for all things urban, south, and mainstream European. As the phrase, To Get Away From It All implies, holidays are often about a perceived suspension of reality. More often than not unpleasant living and working conditions are confused with universal reality, and internal quasi-reservations like the Highlands become literally an un-real fantasy land. When Johnson and Boswell made their famous trek to the Inner Hebrides, their mixture of laughter-eyed play-acting and genuine concern for the people they encountered was an unusually sophisticated response to the Highlands as a place where people actually live.

Adding a further twist is a parodoxical attachment of luxury to the place of the Great British Escape. The Highlands are also very much about a Gentry class who shoot in rich coloured tartan and tweeds, who enjoy the expense of catching and eating salmon, and who drink whisky from crystal. T. S. Eliot, after a car-ride south from Neil Gunn's house in Inverness, spoke accurately and metaphorically in his only Scottish poem, 'Rannoch, near Glencoe,' when he said: 'here the patient stag / Breeds for the rifle.' Venison, one can rest assured, will be on the menu on our own version of the Orient Express, that luxury steam train which creaks expensively up the exotic Mallaig line. I have noticed, too, that the highest concentration of Scotch shops in London are to be found on pricey Regent Street and Knightsbridge. Royalty is implicated in this of course – Windsor has the highest concentration in England of gift shops for tartan and Scottish woollens.

Whisky advertisements seem very much attached to a Scotch Great Britain, too. The adverts for Bell's Old Scotch Whisky are particularly apposite because, perhaps naturally enough, they explicitly present images of Scotland as *the* context for their product. One of especial interest to my admittedly literature-biased sensibility is one which features an interestingly stocked book-shelf. On this shelf, apart from the books, there is a brass microscope, a post card of the Forth Rail Bridge, a souvenir rock sample of white syenite from Lairg, and a book mark inscribed with a thistle, with the words 'The Very Best from Scotland.' The book-mark also has the lion rampant drawn on it. Presumably unintentionally, the lion's head is obscured by a cut-crystal glass placed on top of it. The glass is filled with, yes, Bell's Old Scotch Whisky, and the open bottle is on the shelf, too.

But what are the books on this Scotsperson's book shelf? As the hardware might suggest, this is the bookshelf of one who is interested in the concrete, in the history of Scottish achievement, and in doing practical physical things, or at least giving the impression that he is interested in these things (why do I assume that it's a man's bookshelf?). The books are not what we might normally call fiction, except for a two volume version of Walter Scott's poem sequence, *Marmion*. Trevor Royle has called the plot of *Marmion* 'torturous and contrived,' and the background to it is that famous Scottish victory, the Battle of Flodden Field. Aside from the question of his capabilities, Scott is also, of course, the most notorious unionist in the current Scottish canon.

When we look at the other books, however, despite this minor Scott, here is a country of achievement. The books include Adam Smith's *Wealth of Nations*, biographies of James Watt, the nineteenth century physicist James Clerk-Maxwell, and John Logie Baird. *Penicillin* by Sir Alexander Fleming completes the scientific collection, but we still have other lessons in history. Livingstone, alumnus of Strathclyde University when it was known as Anderson's College, has his last journals published by John Murray of London. It's proud we should be that, before the 'Africans' knew where they were, Livingstone had discovered most of their continent.

What we have in this advert then, is a sharply focused version of 'The Very Best from Scotland.' The remaining 'histories' more or less fall into line with this. The book on Dr Macleod is a biography of one of the great lights of the Church of Scotland who was, incidentally, a very keen supporter of the imperial project to send missionaries abroad (though, in fact, there is a debate now as to exactly what of substance the missionaries brought with them: new medicine or new diseases). Another book which reminds us that we are talking about Scotland itself, not just innovators in Scotland, is the history of Old and New Edinburgh. The need to represent a cultural seperateness legitimised by a sense of tradition is amply satisfied by a *History of Curling*.

Scotland, represented here until about 1945, seems to have been symbolised in the most extraordinary way here. I am not suggesting that *The Wealth of Nations* is not an important text in the philosophy of economics, or that penicillin didn't have a revolutionary effect on Western society. What this advert does, the reason why I have discussed it today, is to present a short-hand for Scottish Achievement which is sending out the most biased and complacent of messages. It is important that we are only seeing the Spines of Books – this advert can name-drop without having the burden of understood except in the crudest terms what these books are really about. Works like *The Wealth of Nations* can be used for the most dubious of purposes: so much so that it has become a text to be avoided by the left simply on the shorthand of the rightwingers who have hi-jacked it. Thatcher and the other leading Scots of our time – Forsyth and the postal box number that calls itself the Adam Smith Institute – are living testimony of this. We will wait and see how Major incorporates Scottish Values into his softly softly monetarism.

The very fact that these post-union books are mostly biographies shows that here in sub-Scotland we have a History of Great Men, not a History of the Scottish people, or anything near it. That most of the Scottish people have been politically and culturally impotent for the span of years that this advert represents makes Bell's phrase 'The Very Best from Scotland' intrinsically qualified. What Scotland? By appealing to a pride in partial achievements, many of which are implicated in British Empire, this advert wants to have its Dundee cake and eat it too. It would have us believe that Scotland is a place of Tradition, of Continuity in Success, yet it portrays a time when for most people in Scotland, as even now, the kind of success, the meaning of success, is sharply compromised by the absence of even the most crude form of self-determination. The souvenir rock sample from Lairg, and the postcard of the Forth Road Bridge, are telling us despite themselves that Bell's is a superficial view of Scotland; the symbolism of pride they are supposed to carry is actually undercut by their laughable ephemerality, an ephemerality which isn't even dignified by the self-knowledge of kitsch.

And what of recent history? On the shelf, we have a fairly new study of Charles Rennie Mackintosh, shamefully neglected by Scotland for years, the *Allan Wells Book of Sprinting*, and a book on Scotland's rugby achievements in 1984. The best of Scotland *today*, Bell's are telling us, constitutes little more than a genius at sports. It is true, of course, that Rangers Football

Club is financially the most well-off of British football companies, but as the regular World Cup fiasco never teaches us our actual game is usually only middling-to-poor. But I dread to think what would happen if Scotland's football team actually won a cup. Having finally achieved cosmic perfection what else would there be to do?

Considered in another light, this advert is not only asking us to admire an individualism which works in tandem with larger capitalist forces, it is assuming that we actually do admire them. If we didn't take a certain pride in being the country of Walter Scott, James Watt, and curling, there would be no point in Bell's issuing the advert. That is, this is not only an advert delineating from on high what the Best of Scotland is, it is actually relying on its audience's collusion. Another way of putting it is that we are in some way responsible for this type of relaxed jingoism.

Before I leave this advert, there is one more thing to note. It has next to no imagery connected to the Scottish countryside. This is fairly rare firstly in Bell's adverts which often feature fly-fishing, or at least dirk-like paper knives, and secondly in whisky adverts in general. Recently there has been a new whisky which is being marketed as a cocktail mixer, and it is advertised with the zappy imagery of obviously urban clubs. This, however, has been very much the exception. These possibly definite signs in the world of whisky, which presumably in the course of maintaining its maturity is always some years behind the pack, are indicative of a change in Scottish images away from the Highlands to the lowland cities, towards heavy engineering projects like the Forth Rail Bridge in the post-card and the shipyards, and towards a much more urban-centred sense of what it is to be Scottish. The importance of the Highlands for anyone concerned with Scotland is that what has happened to them may now be happening to the Central Belt.

Though the slogan for the Irn Bru advert, 'Made in Scotland – from Girders,' goes back to well before the current fascination with Scottish cities, it is experiencing something of a renaissance now that the imagery of heavy industry is so popular. Now that heavy engineering itself has been safely discarded in favour of a 'for-the-common-good-of-the-UK' industrial infrastructure, in which the mal-developed peripheries of Wales and Scotland can be played off against each other, a metal sensibility has become the vogue. The manufacturers, Barr's, have made a rather funny television commercial which basically makes a bid for the Cola market by parodying with aplomb the ludicrous iconic intensities of Pepsi and Coca Cola advertisements. Using slap-stick to laugh at the glossy emotionalism of the world of Coke, Irn Bru shows that the American Dream, which is also Love's Young Dream, is in fact the American Joke. Life isn't about wanting to teach the world to sing. Coca Cola of all things isn't the Real Thing. Yet – *Irn Bru is*?

Reality, and that tough if tongue-in-cheek slogan 'Made in Scotland – from Girders', seem to be talking about the same thing. You see, Scotland is a real world, it's really street-wise; it really know's what's what, and it can laugh about it, too. On the face of it, here is an image that finally we can identify with. We are invited to applaud the rejection of American schmaltz, to think ourselves superior to the Yanks with all the ease that just saying the word 'American' involves. And like the Bell's advert, there is no question that we will actually reject this -- Barr's have done their homework. They know that insularity, a macho self-esteem, and the undercurrent suggestion of the steel mill – in an earlier advert the boy who can tie knots in lamp-posts – are exactly what Scots want to be told about themselves. Nevermind that Scots have never been able to fight in unison for their shipyards and heavy plant when they actually had them. But show us a picture of the Finnieston Crane and we all start humming *The Flower of Scotland*. We conspire in the decay of our country, and Ravenscraig and Linwood are not abstract terms, then we celebrate the picturesque value of our ever-prolonged death.

One of the few full-page adverts in the 1990 Mayfest brochure was one for the Rover 400 series. Its slogan, 'Class without the Struggle', is another of those accidental truths that adverts seem to unwittingly dredge up. 'All cars are created equal', the advert begins. 'It's just that some, as they say, are more equal than others'. The advert doesn't push the reminder further of course. That this is a reworking of Orwell's rather famous phrase in his anti-Stalinist fable, *Animal Farm* is not pursued. But this use of language, I believe, *does* require scrutiny. I know this may be a little po-faced, but I don't think adverts are just adverts. This one's first assumption that inequality is 'the way of the world' is not in dispute, but its next assumption – that material inequality must always be the way of the world – has to be questioned. British firms quoting approvingly from, as it were, the mouth of Stalin, are bad enough, but when they seem to find readers of the Mayfest brochure a ready target for this kind of nudge-nudge, wink-wink cynicism we have to ask if they have been given good reason.

Is that what our so-called renaissance of Scottish arts is about, then? Class, without the struggle? Certainly the artists themselves don't seem to think so. The controversy in Glasgow over the District Council's apparently shabby treatment of Elspeth King and the 'Glasgow's Glasgow' exhibition was noticeable for the presence of writers who were highly vocal in conveying their disgust. These issues clearly beg the question 'Who's Glasgow is it anyway?', and there are disquietening reports about Glasgow becoming, as James Kelman has put it, 'a public company having to operate in an expanding free market economy'. Indeed, there may even be a revival of the Enclosures should Glasgow District do as they seem to plan, and sell off parts of Glasgow

Green. Westminster Council have done it with graveyards, and Glasgow seem keen to make a fast buck on land they, too, have allowed to be a place of the dead.

'Class without the struggle' is an apt phrase in another way, though, because I think there has been a confusion of categories in this new celebration of our cities. It goes back to the Irn Bru advert in a sense, because in the new iconography of Scotland, the Scottish sense of capital R Reality, the Scottish Working Class, and the Scottish Urban Experience, seem to have melted into one another – indeed, have almost become indistinguishable. Not only does the reality exclude or cast aspersions on other types of Scottish experience, such as rural or suburban or middle-class life, it actually exploits the working class it uses. In this way, reviews of James Kelman's books never seem to get much beyond marvelling at the 'real Glasgow' he portrays, as if he was merely relating a version of What It Was Really Like To Live in Glasgow in 1989. And of course, praising writers for lamenting the treatment of the workers is often a surrogate for doing anything about the situation itself. The effect of this type of response to our cities and to our own images of those cities, which is not limited to the book review, is once again to cut things down to size, to control, and to limit. The level at which critical discourse is conducted about writers such as Gray and Kelman, with few exceptions, has still to get beyond a kind of Urban Twilight sentimentality and mystification, responses which are not helpful for their audience or indeed for the writers themselves.

The same laxity in critical understanding has surely happened, until very recently, with Edwin Morgan. Of course Morgan loves Glasgow and writes about Glasgow, but his work offers and challenges so much more. For instance, to think of Glasgow writers in even the crudest class terms is almost ignored on the nod because there is, I think, an assumption that to be part of Glasgow, unless you're some kind of yuppy, is to be working class. The fact that Edwin Morgan's writing arises originally, as he has said himself, from a very much middle-class experience seems no matter for discussion. It is enough that he Belongs to Glasgow, and despite his inherent difference he is accepted as an honorary Working Class Glaswegian.

If we go back to the Highlands, we can see the same pattern, and perhaps we should learn from it. The problem is almost as if Scotland is too 'geographical' a country, that to think of Scotland, as the Tourist Board adverts suggest, is to think of countryside or of city life, and once having thought of these, to think very little further. Neil Gunn suffered from this from the moment his first novel, *The Grey Coast*, was published in 1926. Though he went on to write some twenty or so more novels, he was regarded by his own publisher, Cape, as more or less a one-novel-wonder, one of the assumptions being that there was only one novel to be had from the Highlands, and that in any case, Gunn's Gaelic background and writing style disqualified him from writing real fiction: 'We feel that you yourself are perhaps too Gaelic', they wrote, 'too "poetic", to write a strong novel'.

But the strengths of *The Grey Coast* have very little to do with things Gaelic or, in the simplistic sense, even with the landscape: one of the book's main qualities is to be found in the psychologically sophisticated portrayal of Maggie, the centre of the book, as a woman with a mind and sexuality of her own. We might take this for granted now, and of course there can be problems with male authors' female characters, but in 1926 the book was unusual in Scotland for focusing on man's exploitation of women. Catherine Carswell's earlier novel, *Open the Door!*, is an unlikely predecessor, since its characters inhabit the altogether different world of Glasgow Art School, northern Italy, and London, but really that is exactly my point. Without contracting the myopia of sixties' structuralists, it is yet safe to look deeper into the structures, and what we can see as the issues, of novels, without worrying too unduly about Sheer Geography. *Open the Door!* shares with *The Grey Coast* an at times Lawrentian eroticism, and both, as I have suggested, unequivocally concern themselves with women as intrinsically worthy of attention. Again I stress that this is not in itself to be marvelled at, but within the historical context, and what might be called the preceding Scottish literary tradition, it most certainly is. Also, the edginess, the sheer nastiness of *The Grey Coast* is seldom found elsewhere in Gunn, or for that matter in other Scottish novels.

The Grey Coast unfortunately was not the only book Gunn had trouble with for being too 'Highland'. It would be unwise to underestimate the difficulty Gunn had in getting novels published, despite the early success of *Morning Tide*. This, his second published novel, did not appear until the beginning of 1931. Even taking into account Gunn's activities in the writing of drama and short stories, this five-year gap between novels was not for want of material. But even when Gunn was published, the response was generally the same: either he was writing supremely well about the so-called Essential Highland Experience, or he was dabbling rather amateurishly in affairs deemed outside of his ken. I should mention in passing that Gunn's Highlands, indeed like anyone else's, were fundamentally atypical: several books are rooted in Caithness, others in Sutherland, still others elsewhere, and even within these very different regions, the topographical descriptions Gunn gives them are wonderfully various. Also, Caithness, for instance, certainly does not conform to the Glen Coe and Trossachs idea of what the Highlands are: its cultural influences are quite different from those that might be found further south or further west. Even on the simple terms of geography, Gunn as Highland novelist is a designation to be used with ample qualification.

Turning to the other end of Gunn's writing span, I was interested to find that despite the very fine books he now had firmly under his belt Gunn was still finding it difficult to be seen beyond the limitations he had so obviously leaped beyond. His last novel, *The Other Landscape*, which in my view is still underestimated in Scotland in terms of its technically accomplished twisting of the first-person and its W. S. Graham-like interest in language and its limitations, was seen by the *Times Literary Supplement* as confused, misguided, and unintelligible, but, and here is the big but, 'it is most successful in its evocation of a wild, desolate and haunted landscape.' The rule is, If all else fails, praise Gunn's handling of landscape – he is a Highlander after all. If all else fails, praise James Kelman's Glaswegian stroke working class credentials; if all else fails, mention that Nan Shepherd knew the north-east; if all else fails, Edwin Muir did come from Orkney. I am not trying to say that where we live and how we live are not important – a sense of place is a cliché that some how rings true – but I do think that there is a danger that others will not get beyond this, that they will want to sentimentalise it, and that we will want to do the same.

Another good example of the way critics treated Gunn's later work is the *TLS*'s treatment of the 1952 novel *Bloodhunt*, now widely acknowledged as a tense, subtle and humane book, even among those who somewhat perversely see Gunn's creative death occuring in the decade before. Reviewed alongside other books, ie not seen as important enough to warrant its own space, and under the condescending banner, 'Celtic Miscellany', *Bloodhunt* is described as a book with 'humanity, humour and tension, but perhaps not quite enough excitement. A John Buchan escape among the heather may be something of a cliché, but it is what we have come to expect in this type of setting, and its absence leaves a faint disappointment.' Gunn was right to be embittered about London critics (though he occasionally exaggerated the poverty of his reception), but he was also the victim of Scottish philistinism. Though there are a small number of (mostly non-Scottish) notable exceptions – especially Francis Russell, Kurt Wittig, Douglas Gifford, Margery McCulloch and John Pick – in interpreting and recognising Gunn, Scotland itself has neglected or distorted Gunn's achievement. There is no reason to believe that the temporary darlings of our current 'Urban Renaissance' will not be maltreated in the same way, if they are not already being treated so now (the recent volume on Gray, *The Arts of Alasdair Gray*, is encouraging, though). And I must stress that as in novels, so in our history, and so in our culture in general. My own view is that a sense of place will always be stressed where that place is under threat, a sense of community when there is little community left. That is why the ending of the nevertheless enjoyable film *The Big Man*, where folk from the scheme help out the fatally threatened hero, strikes one as only existing in a kind of fairyland fable. *Gregory's Girl* and *Local Hero* are fair films, but they are bitterly unreal and Twilightish, too (perhaps the most accomplished Scottish picture, Bill Douglas's *Childhood Trilogy*, is of course hardly shown in Scotland, though it appears more frequently in England). When we work to make the happy endings in some way earned and real, not work to enjoy only the bitter-sweet of the illusory fable, maybe Scotland will in some way live up to or change its awful myths. Scotland would be made of girders, in one sense at least, if Scotland actually existed.

Note: this essay is based on a paper delivered at the opening conference of the Centre for Scottish Cultural Studies, University of Strathclyde, 'Images of Scotland', in October 1990.

KENNETH WHITE

The Nomadist Manifesto

I suggest we look first to Southern Siberia, in the second millennium B.C., the far-eastern point of paleolithic civilisation. The tribes were beginning to settle down into societies based on a productive economy, itself based ultimately on the invention of bronze strong tools and weapons, full stables, harvesting. By the middle of the second millennium, the Bronze Age had reached its peak of development, and people were apparently ensconced, once and maybe for all, in comfort and prosperity – but it was just at that moment that several tribes dropped out and *turned nomad*. Which meant extensive movement rather than sedentary business, dispersion among nature rather than the huddling round social edifices, an adventure in space rather than the security of codes.

If it began in the region of the Altai around the 6th century B.C., it soon spread throughout Asia until it became the very substratum of the continent, a perpetual threat, and an incomprehensible presence, to the bureaucracies.

I am not proposing that we turn ourselves into Mongols. I am simply suggesting that something similar is happening today.

At the very peak of industrial civilisation, a discontent has manifested itself, a discontent that has not merely run itself down into quiet desperation. It is as though civilisation were, to say the least, badly in need of breathing space.

A typical voice is that of Antonin Artaud (*Letter to the Rectors of all European Universities*):

> Europe is slowly becoming mummified under the bandages of its frontiers, factories, tribunals and universities. The frozen Mind snaps between the metallic vices that tighten on it. The fault lies with your mouldy systems, your logic . . . You know nothing at all about the Mind, you are ignorant of its most hidden and most essential ramifications, those fossil prints so close to our origins, those traces we can sometimes pick up on the most obscure layers of our brains.

Artaud, grandiloquent, hysterical, at times almost or totally inarticulate, carried in his body-mind a desire that not only made society unbearable but showed up the mass of discourse (artistic, intellectual) of that society as utterly futile. What he looked to, beyond a crisis that would mean either death or an extreme purification, was a culture (defined as a subtle way of understanding and practising life), based on 'metaphysical' grounds, that would allow man, no longer as social individual, but as concentrated point in a cosmic field, to enjoy 'the poetic state, a transcendent state of life.'

It is towards a culture of this kind that the nomad revolution is, in the midst of obscurities and aberrations, evolving.

The ghost that is going around at the present moment is a ghost of eudemonism, its expression going from the plaintive howl of insatisfaction to a heraclitean flow of life that leaves all problems to the dustbin of history. This 'spirit' is carried by a floating group of marginals, intellectual nomads, dionysiacs, evolving on ground that lies beyond what we might call the half-way house of the established Underground, and it is contagious, attracting to it more and more young and fluid body-minds that constitute the foam of a very deep wave. The activity of this group can take various forms, from *anachoresis* to direct confrontation with the forces of repressive order, but it is united in its desire to beak up, break out of, the old conjugation, and by its allegiance to flux, relativism, multiplicity. It has its own gestures and at least the beginings of its own language.

2

It is at the level of language, and hence of logic, that the debate must, ultimately, be situated, for ecstasy needs a basic logic if it is to be permanently high and not degenerate into sentimentality. Which is to say, in other words, that the movement we are concerned with, if it is to maintain the integrity of its emotion, needs seminal texts and diamond-books, beyond the mass of 'literature'.

The logic which Artaud incriminates as the fundamental factor of sclerosis and sterility, leading to an impotence to possess life, is a Greek invention and goes back to the time when Greece was moving out of its primal phase and into that of the city-state. Heraclitus is still speaking an archaic, though desacralised, language, in which man as subject does not particularly distinguish himself, involved in the rolling, contradictory earth. But with Socratic man and his demonstrative skill, an entirely different type of discourse is in function, with man as holder-of-discourse adopting an entirely different status. He perhaps 'is' less, in the sense that he has separated himself from the whole, the *en kai pan*, but he is logical, which gives him *authority*, and he is objective, which gives him *knowledge*.

It was discourse of this type that a twentieth century poet (Hofmansthal, in

the Chandos letter) experienced as a revolting mass of 'decaying mushrooms';
it is discourse of this type that still abounds in assembly-halls and universities;
and it is against discourse of this type, and against the authority and
knowledge that it carries, that the nomads, that is, those who do not
speak, think or live according to this logic, revolt. They revolt, more or
less articulately, in the name of that lost 'being'.

'To sum up', writes André Régnier at the conclusion of a well-reasoned
book (*The Misfortunes of Reason*) on the rise of analytic reason and its
slowly appearing inadequacy, 'our logical thought characterised by the use
of analytical discourse and formal reasoning arose in answer to the need
for perfect knowledge of a world beyond the senses, within the historical
framework of a society emerging from tribalism and in a milieu of intel-
lectuals with moral and legal preoccupations.' We might say that the logic
now in process of formation, which is liable to be characterised by a more
synthetic type of discourse, will be born out of presently expressed needs for
more harmonious living, more perceptive awareness, a more sensuous world,
within the historical framework of a megalopolitan economy, with backward
reference to tribalism (if only as intermediary image, as indicative of a more
organic social system), and in a milieu of intellectual outlaws.

Certainly this new logic will not come into action overnight. Charlatans
and false prophets abound, and there are experts of the academic or the
entertainment industries round every corner ready to turn every intuitive
flash, every fluid gesture, into a dogmatism or a show. As Régnier
says 'It is no doubt useful today to work at possibilities lying beyond
analytic thought; it is certainly necessary to combat at all times crooked
thinking.' Warning against the intellectualist and illiterate mush which
is liable to come in the wake of analytical reason, Régnier says that
what must be looked for, in the absence of logical rigour, is 'that kind
of formal quality which thought acquires when it is gathered together
into one single intuition.' That is almost a definition of poetry, as we
understand it.

3

Poetry, as an archaic activity of the human mind, dismissed by Hegel in the
progressive nineteenth century (see the *Aesthetics*) as a thing of the past, no
longer meeting the highest intellectual demands, may require some defence in
these post-hegelian times when, for example, the massively productive human
sciences may seem to some hasty minds to be on the point of eliminating

literature altogether. And yet, the smallest fragment of real poetry still contains more human (and cosmic) sense and more living inspiration than a whole library of human science. As Theodor Roszak says (*Where the Wasteland Ends*):

> Volumes of hotly dissenting humanist opinion pile up on the bookshelves, brilliant critiques of reductionism, mechanism, behaviorism, structural-functionalism: daring revisions that finally break through, with great self-congratulations, to some minor human truth that Shakespeare or Sophocles long ago salted away in a casual epigram and would never have imagined needing to document or defend. Strange, is it not, how we now have whole libraries of heavy research in the humanities and social sciences . . . that add up to less wisdom, less living insight than many of our youth can find in the words of illiterate primitives like Black Elk.

Certainly, the poet will be aware of the knowledge of his time – he will be much more interested, though, in pure science than in 'human science' – but in his poetic work he evolves in an area of sentient ignorance which, rightly configurated, can become a whole field of cool illumination that no knowledgeable discourse can provide.

4

The nomadic substratum we have referred to, inaugurates its movement at all levels, from the emotional to the psychic to the political. The lack of coherence, partly because of the sheer breadth of scope, is obvious.

One of the principal aims of Surrealism was to find a coherence, in the shape of myth: a myth that might also be a programme. In this Surrealism, although it was the most consequential attempt on the European scene, and remains the first concerted sign of the great drift, cannot be said to have succeded. Too much of a mere city phenomenon, it lacked perhaps an earthing, a grounding, and tended to tie itself too closely to the terms both of psychoanalysis and Marxism. Whereas, as Kostas Axelos writes (*Horizons of the World*), 'to extract the truth from Marx and Freud – as from Marxism and psychoanalysis – would be to bring them back to a more fundamental errancy.'

Describing this errancy, J. F. Lyotard in turn (*A Drift Away from Marx and*

Freud) writes:

> It's not one shore we're leaving, but several at once. And it's not
> an individual, nor a collection of individuals that has embarked, but
> rather, as with Hieronymus Bosch's ship, a collection of fools, each
> fool the exaggerated part of a normal basis, with libido invested in
> some corner of the body, all those fragments placed side by side for
> a voyage without a goal, a collection of fragments that never reaches
> unity because of its drifting, this drifting through various landscapes
> and times giving resonance now to this fool's pulsion, now to that.
> Not a fragmented body, since there will never anything but fragment,
> and since there will never be a body, this errant collection being
> the very affirmation of non-corpus. The plural, the collection of
> singularities, that's what the powers that be, the Kapital, the law
> of value, personal identity, the University, responsibility, family and
> hospital constrain and repress. So, shoreless drifting – in honour of those
> damned. The Odyssey displaced not the polymorphy of Ulysses gathered
> and totalised in a return home, which will be the model of hegelian
> dialectics and all bourgeois-socialist thought and practice. Rather the
> great drift on the spot with fragments knocking against one another, as
> in the *Ulysses* of Joyce.

In the same text, Lyotard speaks of an 'oceanic-sismo-graphic sensitivity' and
of a 'drift of desire', then goes beyond the heterogeneous hotch-potch and
the culture-collage of his ship-of-fools towards the delineation of something
like a goal (although it is not *aimed* at, but forms itself out of the creative
chaosmos like Nietzsche's dancing star) when he writes: 'another libidinal
disposition, still nebulous, difficult to distinguish, is shaping itself out,
standing in a relationship to that of *Kapital* that is neither dialectic
nor critical.'

It is this new 'disposition' which we are out to contour and delineate. A
world, a culture in the making, is what we are concerned with, beginning, as
suggested above, at the emotional level (libidinal unrest), moving through new
configurations of the senses, and of sensuous material, until we come to the
cool reaches of a logic. That is the whole way.

5

Norman Brown (*Life Against Death*) sees the relationship of poetry, and the
'subversive group' it forms, in terms of metapolitics, equating in fact poetry
and metapolitics:

To perceive that it all really takes place in one body
is to transvalue the old political categories
to pass from politics to metapolitics or poetry

poetry being for him basically the sense of this 'one body', a sense of
unity beyond the reality-principle and that cannot be programmed. It is the
'logos of union', otherwise dialectics ('dialectics is intellect seeking union
with energy'):

Poetry is the visionary form, or explosion
which overthrows the reality-principle
and transforms the world, just the way it is,
without changing a thing
the transformation is the unification.
These are the fragmentary moments which bring something new
into the world.
Fragmentary moments: there isn't anything we can count on or
accumulate.

*

Poetry is the solvent which dissolves
the vigorous stereotypes of political ideology
the numb automation of political reflexes
the somnambulist gravity of literal believers.
These are the obstructions to be dissolved

*

The primal Logos is the poetic Logos
and the Logos of unification is poetry

The transition, if transition it can be called, from this metapolitical motivation
and inspiration to ecological consciousness, is immediate. The sense of 'unity
and one body implies a re-examination of man's relationship to the planet on
which he lives. If Brown defines dialectics (poetry being to his mind the
fundamental dialectic) as the union of intellect and energy, ecology might
be defined as the union of economy and energy – human economy and the
energies of the planet. As Howard T. Odum says ('Energy, ecology and
economics'): 'Instead of the confusion that comes from western civilisation's
characteristic educational approach of isolating variables in tunnel-vision

thinking, let us here seek, a common sense overview which comes from overall energetics' – the aim now, necessity, being the changeover from a boom and bust economy of growth to an economy of non-growth and steady energy flow (a state that to the orthodox economist will seem like death, just as its psychic counterpart seems so to the orthodox psychologist), and the question being whether or not it is already too late:

> Has the human system frozen its direction into an orthogenetic path toward cultural crash, or is the great creative activity of the current energy-rich world already sensing the need for change? Are alternatives already being tested by our youth so they will be ready for the gradual transition to a fine steady state that carries the best of our cultural evolution into new, more miniaturised, more dilute, and more delicate ways of man-nature?

6

It is these 'delicate ways of man-nature' that the new movement is trying to tread, often stumbling through undergrowth, often losing its head in confusion, but still following out the path. It begins, not with discourse, nor with discourse directed at discourse, but with a consciousness of the body, which is why Reich tends to be more to the fore than Freud, but the body itself is something more than a psycho-physical entity, it is part of, it is at one with an open system, and the evolving consciousness of this open system requires to be formed. It is not a question of piling up, *in*formation *about* the cosmos or whatever ('research') but of achieving *en*formation *within* the cosmos ('poesis'), the realised totality being a unity of ero-cosmos-logos. The concrete, rightly perceived, analysed, takes us to the 'abstract'.

Referring to the logic which is the third term of the trilogy evoked above, and which it is the task of the new consciousness to evolve, to enform, Kostas Axelos (*Horizons of the World*) writes:

> The resources of traditional and dialectic logic being too poor, we have to look for a logic – beginning by taking existing logic off its hinges – that is the logic of a polyvalent and open game, a logic that accounts for what is accountable, respects the unaccountable, and can also penetrate some secrets of the mythological.

or again:

A speculative thinking that didn't devote itself to vain speculation, but to a historico-meditative examination of world-thought, might evolve a global and polyvalent logic which, linked to poetry and *praxis* would, as a questioning and fragmentary system, go beyond all closed or artificially open logic and dialectic, articulating another language.

When Axelos describes further the open and polyvalent game or world-play referred to above:

> To experience the play-of-the-world is to experience radical Nothingness — beyond all nihilism and without making nothingness a mediation of being. A thinking that would be quieter, more precise and more distant than all existing methods and doctrines, inspiring quieter, more precise and more distant human-posthuman beings might seize and experience the All — in its fragmentary plenitude — as Nothing.

he is speaking in terms that evoke the 'East' (Buddhist, Taoist, Shivaite) rather than the 'West', and this suggests the idea that the new *anthropos* which may deliver us from our civilisation is, within the West, returning to an Asiatic substratum, such as Nietzsche evoked in *The Birth of Tragedy* where he saw such a substratum under-lying Greek civilisation and concentrated in the figure of Dionysos.

Nietzsche in fact looked forward to a meeting of East and West (see *Human All-too-Human*) that would solve the 'enigma of the world':

> I imagine future thinkers in whom the perpetual agitation of Europe and America will associate with asiatic contemplation . . . such a combination will lead to the solution of the enigma of the world. Meanwhile, critical free minds have their mission to break down the barriers that prevent the interpenetration of men.

— he himself being one of those transitional 'free minds', not yet enjoying, except in brief moments, the harmony he envisaged beyond the criticism.

There have been, there will be casualties. There have been, there will be enclosures.

But the roads, despite everything, are open once again.

KATHLEEN JAMIE

The Autonomous Region

The poems need a bit of explanation. In 1989 I set off for Tibet with a photographer friend called Sean Smith. We had a contract from Bloodaxe and an open brief. By the time we got through Pakistan, over the Kunjerab Pass and across the Takla Makan desert, the student demonstrations were growing. The authorities, unnerved, were refusing Westerners access to Tibet. We ended up on the border in Gansu province, which is still very Tibetan, when the Tiananmen Square massacre took place.

The journey was very affecting – bus and train rides 3 days long, grey deserts, steppes, mountains. On the way I 'met' two characters: Fa Hsein, and Princess Wenchen. Though these were both real historical people, I used them in the poems. Fa Hsien was a Buddhist monk of the 4th Century who left his native China and travelled for 14 years through India. Wen-ch'eng is the woman credited with bringing Buddhism to Tibet, c. 640 A.D. A princess of the Chinese court, she was married to the king of Tibet and travelled to join him in Lhasa. Legend has it that the sun-moon mountain near Quinhai Lake is so called because there the princess broke her 'sun-moon' mirror. The sun-moon is a symbol of the harmony of opposing forces, like yin-yang, and to break such an item puts Wenchen, to my mind, on a par with Eve, or Pandora. She took with her to Tibet certain other things unknown in that place: literacy, beer, glass and silk.

The princess breaks the sun/moon mirror

As if a city child knows his heart
can stand no more of this awful thudding
and in a cellar stale and hot
black and breathy
as his granny's lap
escapes his mother's grasp
and makes by alleys and deserted wynds
to the splintering gates
hears the roar
knows all's lost
so opens them.
　　'What will I own' says the princess,
　　surveys her perfect world
　　soothed in winter like a pearl.
　　'A life thrown round my shoulders
　　luxurious as fur; my heart twitches
　　like a dreaming cat.'
Dear maid running
with sodden clothes clung to her like children
whose rain-soaked face is like a sister's
whose company is a clear pool
on a deep and secret river
grasp each other horrified as flowers
and cannot even yell above the wind
sees the mirror smashed at the princess' tiny feet
and on her lips
the beginnings
of a terrible
and mischievous
smile.

The Princess Wenchen travels to Lhasa

Fine horsewomen, both, and a long time travelling.
Wenchen bends low and adjusts the stirrup.
Something tells her this is the border:
a breath of night-wind from the dark and jagged mountains,
a circus of secrets in the valley at her feet.

Nights, and the tents glow in a river bend,
the keepers of secrets
together in cliques –
master brewers growing merry round a camp-fire;
thin faced glass-makers trickle river sand
between their fingers,
the silk-workers guard their covered baskets.
And Wenchen could read the marks of darkness.
O rumour, they have no beer paper script.
Sometimes she wonders
what kind of place it is she's going,
kicks the horse and turns down before nightfall.

Like the others, she talks these days most about the future.
Out in the night they're starting to communicate;
secrets revealed & revealed among themselves.

The travels of Fa Hsien

His bed is hard, his hands, his smell
a travel-musk of months through teeming villages.
The walls of course are stained, the sheet
he almost envies: old, plain.

He rises, ties his top-knot, wanders
to the boiler-room, with his
double-happiness thermos flask,
noting
    every vessel can be broken, filled,
and he is empty, these days. Not old
as the sun-lines round his eyes suggest
which eyes have seen:
many things out of strong places
etcetera. And who knows what his robe conceals:
tattoos, a bleeding heart.

*

There's roads and there are one-horse towns
and any climb out of hamlet, gorge or wilderness
he looks in wonder,
to fellow-travellers he replies:
what wisdom have I gathered? none!
'That's my tuppence-worth,' walks on.
'Throw it in a ditch and walk unburdened.'

And also in the ditch, a dog, days dead, ignored.
'I've lied, and vowed at umpteen altars,
and know I can be
utterly deceived,
perhaps still am.'

At the thin black line of shade at a truckstop
while they fix the fan-belt
and there's no water
he'll bring out yarrow-stalks, divine.
And sometimes, walking alone he finds
the centre of his being, flinches,
   for it's nowt
   but an alms bowl.
Waiting at a roadside, he scratches the dust
with a stick, finds: more dust.
In the hot shade of some godforsaken Xingjiang bunkhouse
remembers the river and the fish.
(o monk whither do you wander?
to garner wisdom & bring scripture home)

*

Swags and swathes of hills billowing o
as a child he dreamed of sailing; the sailing hills;
he hears his heart shanty and shepherds
call like bo'suns.
The prayer-flags yearn like full-rigged ships
to quit this witness, earth. He knows
already he's too far slipped
to make the leap ashore,
aye, its strange quiver; and he knows
himself an arrow already shot the bow.
He cries, tells himself, as if he didn't know
it's worth it, worth it, worth it.

BOB COBBING

from **Life, the Universe and Everything**

Binoculars can show you
where the brow of
the next hill is
but not what lies beyond
insight not eyesight
that is what you need
though succeeding so well
in solving problems
that you run out of
problems to solve
is a Pyrrhic victory
if one day a doctor
finds a universal nostrum
for all disease bang
goes the medical profession
a single stroke of insight
into word frequencies in linguistics
error bursts in transmission
of messages turbulence
galaxy clusters fluxations
of the stock market the
level of the river Nile
could blow up a circuit board
genuine chaos that
brings you down to earth
oh yes we can predict the weather

accurately provided it doesn't
do anything unexpected
on the island of Corfu
there's a superstition that
if you see a praying mantis
it brings you either good
luck or bad luck
depending on what happens
the same problem run on
two different makes of
computer leads to
two different answers
one would be telling us
there's a heatwave coming
the other would be predicting
a blizzard if you
thought computers were
infallible think again.

Two poems from **Ring Ding the Machine**

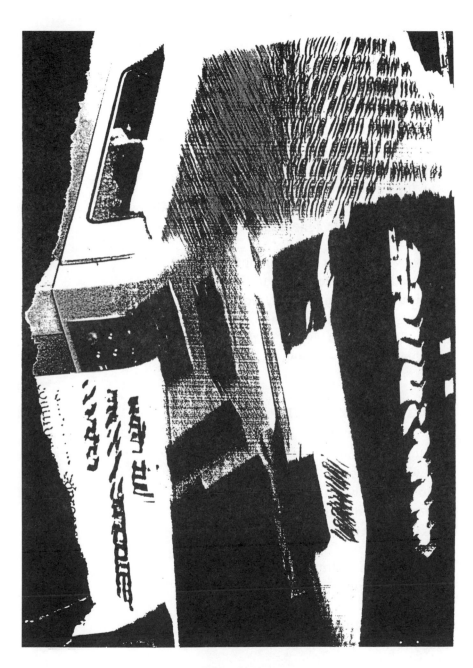

Note: these poems were created for performance.

ELIZABETH JAMES

Capricorn

And so I'm left with what I left with, a half-
recognised scent filling the room, a moment
before you'd softly offer that vivid blossom
drawing us down the midnight lane to sit
among the churchyard ghosts like children almost
overtaken first by vague desire

for we were neither children, nor overtaken.
Tethered like constellations to their turn,
the dead to one bruised turf, we shared a breath
of balsam, stayed half-strange, and after dreaming
slept. So the glittering eye of the goat
revolves morosely around its splintered post.

'Erat hora': 3 a.m.

I still don't know
if it was in or out
of love I fell, when you
pattered naked into the kitchen
looking for Alka Seltzer.

Your real body, strip-
lit, beyond thought –
and what held me transfixed:
the fascinating risk
that you were going to be sick.

Well, it was quickly over.

KEITH JEBB

the green man

my face, wiping off against the couch-
grass, anyway lies on the road to winter,
the moon's milk-bottle-top coin above
frost-candied houses, the sugar-fine snow.

Oil's pretty, its slime-spectra on puddles,
black ooze on the road like the first
spasm of a painting. You see a hand
signing, making shadow faces on a wall,

the heads of mammals, birds with
stubby wings and something too much like
yourself in profile. Horsechestnut leaves
like dripping hands, apples like breasts,

tree-shapes always like women, gnarled
crones or lithe young women? How
the robin is cheeky, like a child.
You are an eyeball floating along

a country lane, drinking down the light,
its ripples and surfs of colours, coming
into itself on the retina. In a coppice
across a sock-wet morning field

brambles cling, snag and scratch
lovingly; nobody sees you. The sky
paddles through muddy furrows, cows
shift nervelessly in the mist;

around you, the one point of composition,
the lens that every painting seems
to strain for. You inhabit the world
as water inhabits your body.

But some days the sun cuts your figure
black from the ground, like a following
grave; or at night, that other double,
the blank moon, wavering in a puddle.

A blank puddle, shaking the moon.

TOM McGRATH

Blythswood Square

The Square is deserted now.
No cars parked outside the RAC Club.
The meters look lonely.
Only daisies and sparrows
on the office workers' lunchtime grass.
Myself at my solitary window.
Making a top-floor din
with some Sonny Rollins jazz.

How many different processions and banners,
celebrations, protestations
have I seen beat drums and march,
shout themselves on time
around this place of business
(one kind or another), Blythswood Square.

Yesterday the Orangemen,
their kids in sashes,
weighed down by accordions;
a week ago the nurses
in full uniform, red white blue,
a length of capes demanding
something more than Florence Nightingale;

a CND march, pathetic in one corner,
oh, that so few should care,
the same few, doubtless, who marched
to make real the pain of Chile,
vain hope in Glasgow
where even oil or Belfast
can't raise coherence;
the students, looking like thousands,
long-haired through the rain
demanding higher grants – how I long
to see them march for a change in curriculum,
and how, in the hard face of religious bigotry
have I longed for the flutes to play
a song of unification and of you –

the blood and shattered brick of Belfast,
the shattered skulls, the lonely graves of Ireland
that have no name –

I move back from the window pane
which separates me from the Orange marchers.
My impotence like cancer in the back of my brain.

c. 1972

Transport Museum

Pale, dried up, torn
like driftwood,
except it lies
in the rubble
of the South Side of the city,
remains of a fence,
another splinter
from the once was

Times gone by
sing the Glaswegians
and a silly smile
comes over their collective faces:

'Mind the steamie? Oh, yon was great!
Those wur the days! There's no denying it.'

I pick up the piece of wood,
just for a moment indulging the flash
of a memory of boyhood,
then throw it down again
so that it stirs up some dust.
This would have been
a great place to play.

The woman with blue eyes
who walks beside me
notices but does not say anything.
She's from Belfast.
I wonder what she's thinking.

There are five of us
exploring the vastness
of the abandoned site,
looking into its future.

Only I am from Glasgow.
I alone am from Glasgow.
Alone, I am from Glasgow.
From Glasgow, alone.

Surrounding tenements
look down on us
and seem to me like
old acquaintances.

'That balcony up there. That used to be the stables . . . '
When the transport was horse-drawn. Old photographs.
'Oh, yes. Very fine.'
Funny how they always seem to know
when something is nice to look at.
'Unfortunately it will have to come down.'
'Structurally unsound.'
'Oh, yes. A hazard.'

We look over a wall
to a rusting railway track.
A grey wagtail flashes yellow
as it zigzags off.
I start to mention it
then keep my mouth shut.
What does a grey wagtail
have to do with anything?
It's not a building,
it's not capable
of becoming
a theatre space.

Inside, stagnant water of the after-Mahabaratha,
the iron column the designer
insisted had to be there.
Peter Brook's directions
still hanging in the air.
Blue-fashed Krishna and the Elephant God.
Old tramlines in the stone.

2.

Outside we group around a car with meteoric logo flashing
1990 Glasgow European City of Culture.
A wee man passes, bunnet on head, big wife on arm
a couple from an *Evening Times* cartoon (Gall's Grin).
Taking the motto in he snarls en passant –
'European City of Culture? Don't talk tae me aboot culture!
Pit some public toilets in the Queens Park,
then you can talk about effin culture.'
And he walks on down the road.

'He's absolutely right, of course,' says the designer.
'Glaswegians are such wits,' says the whizz kid.
And I am from Glasgow. I alone am from Glasgow.
I am from Glasgow. Alone.

'Can we give you a lift, Tom? We're going back into town.'
No. That's alright. I'll take the tram.

As I wander on up past the Azas video and the kebab shop
I see an old Indian in a turban and loose-fitting clothes,
his long grey beard pointing down to the streets of Glasgow.

1988

HUGH McMILLAN

Some Scottish problems resolved

1. The mystery of Pictish symbol stones
  and the origin of the Saltire.

(Some people say that the Saltire was adopted as the flag ⟨
Scotland when Oengus, King of the Picts, saw the cross ⟨
St Andrew miraculously inscribed across the sky above h
victorious army.)

Retainer of King Oengus:
          Fuck me, will ye look at that.
          Ah hevnae seen an arrangement o clouds like that
          since we spottit the wan that looked
          like a zebra on a surfboard –
          ye ken; the thing we carve on a' the stanes.

King Oengus himself:
          Christ, yer right.
          Come an we'll adopt it as oor national motif.
          It'll be easier to scratch on wa's
          an a fucking sight less confusing
          for ethnologists.

HUGH MacDIARMID

Letter to William Jeffrey

16 Links Avenue
Montrose

24/12/28

My dear Jeffrey

Of course I shouldn't have quoted your letter without your
permission: but a private letter of Thomson's stung me into a
fury. I should be extremely sorry if the result had been harmful
to you in any way – but, at the same time, I must say that one
of the things that has hurt me most all these years, and one of
the things that plays into the hands of people like Thomson, is
the fact that for one reason or another none of my friends will
openly range themselves alongside me. I grant it isn't easy to do.
To maintain my own stand involves me in sacrifice enough. But
if instead of having to fight singly I'd half-a-dozen others with me
equally determined we'd win through. As it is, I'm being frozen
out – Scotland is denying me even the barest livelihood. There
isn't a single Scottish paper I know of that will give me even an
ordinary reportership (though a daily paper reporter gets nearly
double what I get here for doing the same work – and a hanged
sight less of it). What the upshot's going to be, I don't know. I
suppose I'll have to clear out. In any case, there's two things I
won't do – 1/ shut up as long as I can give tongue; 2/ compromise
with the parasites.
　　At the same time, mind, I'm not reproaching you or being stu-
pidly self-righteous and moralising in the slightest. The difference
between Thomson and all the other hangers-on – and you – to me

lies singly in the fact that you have done work of consequence; they haven't. That makes all the difference in the world to me; and is the basis so far as I am concerned of a regard which will not be altered one way or another by anything you either do or don't do for me or to me. Our opinions and lines of action may differ as much as they like – that can't alter an esteem which is based on quality of mind as shown in work done.

But – having said that – I am all the more free to say that I bitterly regret that – not you alone but many of my friends find themselves unable to come out on my side, and thus prop-up the nincompoops who must be cleared out of the road altogether before anything of any real value can be done. It was inexcusable to publish part of a private letter – but is it any more excusable to praise a man's position in private and allow his traducers to have it all their own way in public?

Do not imagine that I am asking for help in all connections, however, either from you or anyone else. Far from it. I am only posing the question alongside that of impotence – betrayal, as an essay in ethics – an academic speculation? As I have already said I do not judge on moral grounds, and it doesn't matter a scrap to me what any one's ideas of honour and dishonour or anything of that kind are – all I'm concerned about in the last analysis is intellectual status, and artistic worth.

I know you'll forgive me for printing your name and a bit of your letter – and you know I'll forgive you for not printing them yourself – and there we are, and I'm able to wish you (and do most heartily) all the compliments of the season and every good wish for the coming year.

Yours

C. M. Grieve

HUGH MacDIARMID

from the MS of **The Kind of Poetry I Want**

All that is good goes on light feet.
It is with what I seek as with
A superb car, one of the world's masterpieces of engineering,
Attempting the land speed record on the Salt Flats of Utah,
Shod with special tyres costing about £90 each
   – And how thick, would you think, are the treads?
I asked a man the other day
And he said two or three inches.
Have you made your guess?
Well, let me tell you.
About the thickness of a fly's wing.
A mere wafer of special material,
Strong as steel, supple as silk;
Centrifugal force would blow
Anything thicker to smithereens.

JOHN MANSON

Hou Monie Lives Has a Man?

Hid's haurd till gang in Embro yit without mindan o the poems o Sydney Goodsir Smith. Nae langer 'The lums o' the reikan toun/Spreid aa ablow . . . ' as they wir ablow the Castle whan I ferst cam til Embro about forty year sinsyne, nae lang eftir Sydney wrote *Under the Eildon Tree*. Nae langer 'The gaslicht flichtered on the stair', though the stairs ir there. Bit aye 'The streaman cobbles black wi rain', and no juist the cobbles: the shelvin steps at the Post Office or on yir richt as ye gang up the Lawnmarket.

So Late into the Night whilk Peter Russell prentit in 1952 his aye been ma favourite wurk o Sydney's. I hid ma name in for a copie and yuised till wunder whan hid wiud come out, whiy it wisna coman out . . . . Nou I ken about pit affs. Syne it cam, and a fine haunfu it wis, prentit on thick paper, wider nor uswal.

Hid's the buke o Venus, o wumman wha gies or hauds back great favours in the wurds o Santiago in *The Old Man and the Sea*. Hid's the warld o mark Alexander Boyd's great sonnet and the saxteen hunder Alexander Scott. Thrailldom to wemen, langour, loss, pairtin, separatioun, traitorie; faur mair rarely, pais; thir ir the themes o maist o the poems. 'Luve in Fetters' is a guid ensample:

> I
>
> To grien for her, and then,
> The haein dune, to fear,
> E'en i the airms o her,
> The glorie that maun end;
> To see the twynin ere
> The passin's spent –
> Och there
> Is luve in fetters lain.

II

It is I that cry, here
In thir leanan streets
My prison, whar the wind beats
Wi the like lash I bear
Reid on the nakit breist –
To hae you here when I hae nocht
And, when I hae, no fear
The endin o't.

Sydney kent whit he wis writan about, ilka step o the rod is shuir-fitted. In tichtly-ivven Scots verses he pits forrit ilka tim o a feelin, a trith. It taks its place wi ither great luve poems o thae hunder year: Hikmet's 'Ibrahim's Dream in Prison', Vaptasarov's 'On Parting', Montale's 'Dora Markus', Desnos' 'The Last Poem', Eluard's 'Lady Love', Aragon's 'Rooms' . . . the leet will be as lang as wir readin alloos.

I yuised twa lines o 'The Moment' in ma ferst paragraph: they dae nae mair nor pit ye in the picter. In this poem the langour is owre, there is a meenit o pais (tho a bit o oonease about the future).

– And aa the grienan years were lain.

Fowr year leered up like paper then . . . .

Of course this kind o poem didna stert and didna feenish in *So Late into the Night*. In 'The Scaur', frae an earlier buke, *The Deevil's Waltz*, ferst prentit by MacLellan in 1946, Sydney compares the hort dune til his feelins til a seed whilk breers ilka spring in a fine kintra eemage:

There is nae luve, I ken,
Wantan a skaith; but whaur's
The luve can ever ban
I' the weary hours
The bluidy braird o an auld scaur,
Thocht deid, that jags again?

There wis 'The Reid Reid Rose' frae *Cockils* in 1953, and in his last buke wi separate lyrics, *Fifteen Poems and a Play* in 1969, 'Winter Blues' is for him an oonuswallie quaiet poem o laneliness expressit maistly throu monosyllables:

A high cauld room. Winter.
Put coal to the fire.
It's a while to heat a room
Even with coal on the fire.

. . .

There's food and drink for me here
But nane to provide me.
I sup frae a black bottle
Her face far beside me.

Wis this the tap flat in Dundas Street, I wunder, a livan room as big's a
tennis court wi mebbe a couch for a net, posters o *The Wallace* on the waa,
his ain bukes alane on a shelf wi MacDiarmid's, the tane's leanan til yin side,
the tither's til th'ither, a table wi jotters o manuscripts owrelappan ilk ither,
and John Broom's room merkit 'Private' bi the Auk himsel wi virrlek scarts
o his pen?

' . . . the themes o maist o the poems' I said abune. There wir twa chefe
exceptiouns, the ferst and the last. 'Torquemada and the Carapace' hes been
in ma mind aa thae year. I canna link it til the teetle, Torquemada the chefe
judge o Ferdinand and Isabella, bit I can link it til masel.

1

Hou monie lives has a man,
Hou monie faces can
At aince be shawn til men
While at the quick is nane o them
But a bleezan coal
Hapt deep in the saul?

2

Why, like a partan's carapace,
Maun aye a rantan face
Defend the ither nichtit sel
For damn the reason in hevin or hell
Sauf jaggie pride, that greits til ane
But aince – or maybe never, til nane?

I sud say that *So Late into the Night* cam intil the but end o a croft hous in Caithness wi its flagstane flure and open herth and whaur the Bible, Burns and twa illustratit bukes o fushes and burds hid lang hauden swey. And whan I gaed til the University o Aiberdeen twa year bifore, I hid til mak the muve frae auld farrant hens càkkan me til the mort claith, frae weel kent neibours and friens slawly, suddenly intil a burn o bleiter o faces and braw, birlan anonymitie, frae the hauden doun thraill o the awned and the threipit haims on masel intil the grumlie watter o weet broun stour ruits rummlan, sloppin, til the hastie, lauchan facilitie o the weel unkent. Laiter I hid to mak the oonsocht chainge frae the success hauden out bifore me til the 'failyier' I becam, kennan deep doun that I wis richt, anither wey o bein richt, that I wis takkan a lang rod roun til a mair foundit success, I houped!

The last poem, 'Hamewith', is the ither chefe exceptioun. Agane the wurds ir maistly monosyllables, the lines here ir fower or five syllables (aa bit yin), verse til croun ower:

> Man at the end
> Til the womb wends,
> Fisher til sea,
> Hunter to hill,
> Miner the pit seeks,
> Sodjer the beild.
>
> As bairn on breist
> Seeks his first need
> Makar his thocht prees,
> Doer his deed,
> Sanct his peace
> And sinner remeid.
>
> Man in dust is lain
> And exile wins hame.

Dora Markus

from *Bagni de Lucca*, 1929
(Translated from the Italian of Eugenio Montale)

1

It wis whaur the widden pier
striks out at Porto Corsini abune the high sea
and a fyow lane men, aa bit unmovan, pit oot
or pu in thir nets. Wi a waave
o yir haun ye signed til yir ain land
oot o sicht on the faur shore.
Then we followed the canal richt doun til the herbour
o the citie, shinan wi shuit,
in the flat lands whaur a hingan spring
gaed doun, out o mind.

And here whaur an auld-warld life
is mizzled wi a saft
aistren unrest,
yir wurds fleered aa the colours o the rainbow
lek the scales o the chokkan mullet.

Yir unrestiness maks me think
o flittan burds that flee intil lichthouses
on wild nichts:
yir pais is a blizzard tae,
it swirls and disna shaw it,
and its lown whiles are still fyower.

I dinna ken hoo ye're livan, woorn oot,
in yir sloch
o yir hert's airtlessness; mebbe
a handsel gairds ye,
yin ye keep bi yir lipstick,
yir pouder-puff, yir file: a white mous
in ivorie; and sae ye get by!

D. M. BLACK

The Scottish Avant-Garde in the 1960's: A Note

I don't remember, in the 1960's, thinking in terms of a 'Scottish avant-garde'. That suggests a kind of conscious and coherent grouping of like-minded writers or artists. What we had was a remarkably individual poetic scene, in which the only forces that exerted a pressure to conform were political – nationalist and left-wing – rather then aesthetic. It would have taken a brave poet in the Scottish 1960's to vote for the Tories! But we – by which I mean the bunch I happened to know, in our 20's or so in that decade – had no objection either to the most traditional of styles (for example, Robert Garioch's immaculately crafted sonnets in Scots), or to, say, the pioneering typographical constructions of Ian Hamilton Finlay, which were part of the world's avant-garde but not really of Scotland's. Each of the Scottish poets seemed extremely distinctive, and this was as true of the younger poets – I think of Robin Fulton, Alan Jackson, Duncan Glen, Alan Bold, Tom Leonard, Kenneth White, etc – as it was of their elders. There weren't the sort of groupings that one would call 'an avant-garde'.

I see two possible reasons for this. One is that Scottish writers, determined not to be English, either turned to specifically Scottish traditions or languages, or exposed themselves to any of a huge range of influences, from Europe, America or China and Japan. In this they followed the example of that famous anglophobe, Hugh MacDiarmid, whose influence was fundamental to all of us. But – the second reason – MacDiarmid was a mentor without being a model. His great work, the romantic Scots writing of the 1920's, was too far in the past to be a temptation; and his more recent brain-cracking parades of erudition and prophecy could be wondered at but hardly imitated. He shielded us from other orthodoxies without establishing an orthodoxy himself, except, as I said, of a political kind. And in the 1960's those political attitudes, an orthodoxy of revolution, so to speak, were on the whole pretty acceptable to most of us. MacDiarmid's 'Stalinism' was of course already clearly absurd, but it seemed an academic and harmless whim compared with the real, current horrors of the Vietnam War.

One other factor should be mentioned. I have been thinking here of poets, but on a wider scene there were extremely influential figures, very often Americans avoiding the draft, who played a big part in protecting us both from England and from Scottish parochialism. One of the most conspicuous of these was Jim Haynes, who ran the Traverse Theatre in Edinburgh, but there were many others. Perhaps I may pay tribute here to a greatly admired friend of my own, Rick Ulman, an American painter who taught in Dundee in the mid 1960's, to whom I owe an enormous debt for introducing me to the world of then-recent American painting, and to whole realms of sensibility that would not usually have been represented in Eastern Scotland. In a shallow way, we were curiously American-ised. Kenneth White, in *Travels in the Drifting Dawn*, gives a wonderful account of a meeting with Alexander Trocchi ('Joe Torelli') which vividly conveys the flavour of a lot of 1960's life. I like to think we were all individuals and pioneers at that time, not a definable avant-garde, and not even uniformly Scottish, but it will be interesting to know how it appears to those to whom the 1960's are only history.

DAVID KINLOCH

The Apology of a Dictionary Trawler

My interest in Scots stems from a combination of two personal but unconnected circumstances.

Around the age of twelve or thirteen, I stopped writing long, turgid plays about Robert the Bruce and Roman gladiators dying for their Emperor in heroic latin gore and started writing poems about the furniture in my bedroom where I was frequently sick. The turn to poetry was stimulated by the discovery that my maternal grandfather, William Jeffrey (1896–1946), had been a poet. I was also startled to discover that he had written much of his later work in Scots. Shortly afterwards, when I was more able to appreciate the significance, I was fascinated to bear that, as Jeffrey lay on his deathbed listening to a radio programme in his praise, one of the speakers, Hugh MacDiarmid, pronounced that his best work had been in Scots and that the rest was rubbish.

This did not make me rush to discover my grandfather's Scots poems. My grandmother, who lived with my family, never forgave MacDiarmid for his tactlessness and the grudge was harboured with increasing care as the years passed and my grandfather's name fell into obscurity as MacDiarmid became a sweet, if crusty, old genius. To read my grandfather's Scots poems or to linger over them at any rate would have been a little like agreeing with MacDiarmid.

It wasn't until I found myself in Oxford doing a post-graduate degree in French and met Robert Crawford and Bill Herbert that the issue of Scots poetry came up again. By this stage I had read MacDiarmid and, putting family prejudice aside, come to agree with him that my grandfather's best work was written in Scots. But it had never occurred to me to try to write anything myself in Scots until Robert Crawford asked me if I'd ever tried it. My initial reaction was that in order to write it I should at least be able to speak a dialect of it or, at any rate, be much more familiar with Burns and MacDiarmid than I was. My grandfather had a sound rural background and rooted his experiments in Scots within that living framework. In my case, a handful of words here and there plus a dollop of Glaswegian didn't seem a lot to go on. My wiser colleagues however began to produce screeds of synthetic

Scots poetry some of which I found – and still do find – very exciting and frequently hilariously funny.

The nature of this excitement is really what I have been asked to write about for its perpetrators constitute part of what the editors of *Gairfish* have chosen to call the Scottish avant-garde. It might help, however to smooth the hackles this expression will raise – with all its vainglorious connotations – if I try to describe my own attempts to create some of this excitement, the failure of these attempts and how that failure has fed my own recent poetry and in a sense become part of it.

Indeed the term 'Scottish avant-garde' is fraught with difficulty and contradiction. Poets like Crawford and Herbert, however they push forward, are always looking back over their shoulder and write of joy, sexual, emotional, with words we thought irrevocably lost, balancing them like jugglers over the abyss of the dictionary from which they have been pulled. It is a poignant balancing act; if the plates fall the derision will be great. As this is Scotland of course, the derision has been great, even although the plates are mostly still up there. That, however, is another story, or rather part of this one which I prefer to pass silently over.

I began, then, to try to write short lyrics in Scots. Initially I was hampered by the fact that there was no English-Scots dictionary available. Since then I have got hold of William Graham's *Scots Word Book* and still use it frequently. But my main problem was connectives, personal pronouns, all the little words that get you from phrase to phrase. Oh, I found wonderful nuggets in Chambers, then in Jamieson, but I needed a string for my pearls! Was it an' or 'n, uv or o', ah or uh or eh for I? Vowels were a pest. I was pulled one way then another. I could have settled for one relatively consistent scheme but it just didn't sound 'real'. It certainly wasn't 'me' and it didn't sound much like anybody else either.

I was more successful with translations and am still interested in translating into a variety of Scots. Perhaps this is because 'translatorese' is akin to the half-way house my Scots had become, a kind of fluorescent no-man's land where you could make out some very brightly coloured shapes and hear very clearly the exact timbre of the people who stepped into it. And it is this phrase 'half-way house' and associated words and expressions – 'seuil', lytch gate, margin – that helped me to think more clearly about what Scots meant to me, how I could relate to it and to the language of my forbears.

For it seemed to me as I laboured with my dictionary, as I tried and tried to link its words up and make poems, that there was far more poetry in them when I left them in their squat paragraphs than when they swarmed forlornly about my white page looking for some connective to hold onto. And it seemed to me also that this strange, poignant feeling – quite common among Scots writers – that I was more alive in some of these words than in their English equivalents, that I 'knew' them and 'recognised' them as my own even as I came upon them for the first time, it seemed that this too was true and that this truth was perhaps unreachable and inexpressible. Finally, it seemed that the kind of 'Scots' poetry I could write would be an attempt to link these two perceptions up. To say that it was a question of writing poetry without leaving the dictionary makes it sound dry and intellectual. It also simplifies the experience. It is more a question of clothing yourself in the dictionary as you write, of wearing it, of letting its words form the rich loops and pleats of a jongleur's sleeve, of admitting the ordered anarchy of the dictionary into your pen, of welcoming the plurality of its definitions, of surrendering to the dictionary as we once did as children although we have mostly forgotten that experience, and of wearing the insult 'dictionary trawler' as a crown.

It is a matter of admitting the lost and unsayable into your poem and celebrating or at least articulating the loss and unsayability they bring with them. The poetry for me is sometimes in the gap between what is yours to feel and sing and the word that will best convey it, the word that belongs not to you but to a dictionary and to your grandfather's grandfather, the dictionary's ghost. The best word for life is dead. But this can be a joyful experience because it reminds you, the reader, the writer, that you are not a word, not just language, but somewhere beyond it, incommunicable, alive.

What this means in practice for the art of the poet is that his 'Scots' poetry will sometimes not look or even sound like 'Scots' poetry. It will incorporate a great variety of voices and textures, dialects and accents and may even, occasionally, sound like criticism. This kind of poetry is not just about living in the word and helping it to sing or about helping the singer to sing in the word but about *watching* the word *try* to sing and the singer *attempt* to produce a pure note, about the failure of these attempts and the peculiar mixture of joy and sadness this engenders. It involves embracing and using some of the insights of literary theorists, particularly those who have spoken about the divorce that exists between words and the things they represent – an experience Scots are uniquely qualified to talk about. But perhaps most importantly it involves the poet in an attempt to find a language or to choreograph a dialogue of languages appropriate to his or her experience of living in twentieth century Scotland with all its linguistic and social diversity.

DAVID KINLOCH

Gurliwhurkie

'Unforeseen evil, dark, dismal, premeditated revenge. It is scarcely possible to know the origin of terms of such uncouth combination and indefinite meaning.' Jamieson

Habbacraws! The Renfrew Ferry throws up its glass bonnet. She nods. Tonight she sails: blackfisher of the Clyde. Far out beneath the Kingston Bridge an illegal banquet cups its ears and jumping to its feet says: 'Can you hear them? I hear people in the air, but cannot see them. Listen!' We strain (with every pore) until we hear invisible brothers, whole words against our flesh. And they are: greengown, dustie-fute, rinker, rintherout, set, abstaklous, alamonti, afftak, baghash, amplefeyst, let-abee for let-abee. It is dew on Gideon's fleece. It is Homer's bounding, flying and consequently alive words. It is Plato thawing in the Glasgow air. It is the head and lyre of Orpheus. All these and on the deck before us whole handfuls of frozen words, gay quips, some vert, some azure and some or. Shall we fear them then? Take no risks and we'll get no slaps! One of us begins to horde yet warmed between our hands they crane upwards like a baby cham. It's then the gurliewhurkie gets to work: just as we're about to understand their throats are cut. Mump the cuddy, aftercome, falderall and ezle melt on a lover's palm and shout: hin, hin, hin, his, tick, tock, bou, bou, bou, bou, tracc, tr, trr, on, on, on, proddle, proop. Habbacraws! We saw them look back over our shoulders into the water. We saw the words stop bobbing like so many buoys in the waters. We saw the last gleam of dark eyebrows in the water and it said: by-coming, bairnie of the e'e.

Dustie-fute in Mumbles

I get up in the night
And let his voice
Out of the breakwater into light.

Pier upon pier constellate
In the lyre of his memory:
Jetties tensing at the touch of boys' feet
Which echo in the mind like ships
That nudged his severed head, bobbing now
In my swivel chair like a buoy.

Dustie-fute released from the oregon
Pine of Mumbles pier, tells me
Of mushroom anchors, jarrah wood paving
Of Dundee and how at Arromanches,
Locked within mild steel pontoons,
He took the weight of tanks.

Post-Euridice, he has floated in
To tell me of the sex of words
Which looped around his ears
Among difficult Scottish kyles,
Setting 'aucht' upon his lips
'Froe' and 'huzzibaw' in his hair.

He has come to tell me how domestic loss
Placed a cypress in his heart,
Its tongue half-learnt and half-inherited
Which gave fast stories that surged in him
Like lifts, sharp swords that hung above his head.

He has come to tell me of an underwater
Tongue, hippocamp, pure, useless
As the moles and dolphins
Which burrow and porpoise
Only in arcades of pleasure
They bear upon their backs.

Dustie-fute on Rhodope

His tongue is cypress on tiptoe
above a chattel of Ibizan bars
and his uncut nail a carbon wave
against an island sky.

His voice is groves of esh
and hoburn sauch,
his throat the knot-holes of their bark
which pestle the laughter
of a small port's clubs
with the ferryman's light scorn.

His eyes are a boy's chanter,
reedy as remote infantas,
his red and blue chirrups
balance air, lob through
the house-music from the bay.

His back is a woman
turning through the night
and women will turn on him.
His lips are a discus of hyacinth,
vernacular rooting in its fall.

His smile is an accent
stretched by Ciconian hordes
until his limbs cartwheel away,
beche-de-mer, brogue,
caught in girls' hair
which streams in the common
printout of their pain.

Icarus

Somewhere Eskimos are weeping
For failing to bury enough sunlight
In their igloos.
But in Outer-Siberia a man with a bear-skin
Telescope laughs like the steppe,
Detecting the changing smiles of Icarus
At different pitches of the air.

DUNCAN McGIBBON

The Creation of the Garden Boy

No, not places . . . these either, only a conjecture or a mist. Something like the dew, trailing from the place where the canal flowed, a sudden fall behind the great screen of grass that rose beyond the massive girths of the oak trees, erupting at intervals in front of the long, black ironwork fence that ran the width of the garden to the house. Yesterdays grown out and tied back, their greenery fading after the flowers that elsewhere rose sharp as a second against the railings.

Who could note that other space where begonias blaze, fearsome, selfish, heedless of apparitions passing its oblivious bulk? Yet this kind of thing could hardly prevent the little boy shouting at the dumfounded passer-by, 'Have you come to be my dad now?' The imponderable absence of sufficiency; that hard, vital loss of completion, a sense of ending, whirling away with that; that the mist so quick to go, to distract the conscious edge might seem more semblance to this unsayable regret, just for that knowing minute, missing its balm. All this place was so thick with events that the house could not be seen. Nothing so big of course, nothing you might say, that fits, but leafage enough to confuse the unwary who might have gone out not knowing the exact whereabouts that satisfy; too sudden, you see, like a child impetuous to go out, not remembering how many turns away from the established moment, unfinishingly, it must go on. Until looking back under the pallor of light rain, the huge bush of Bougainvillea or rhododendrons all seem another place in that instance. And other people coming along, elsewhere, hearing the sound flow away like water through a plantpot filled with loamy earth.

The day too has canals, though they are mostly a matter to do with wounds, noticeable at low tide, running across places made for greater concentrations of water, such as a beach, where its little narrow strip of mud runs level at the price of vanishing again. Why do voices stop also? Somebody notices that the possiblilities of sadness are numberless and goes on with the dog down to the embankment. Besides hasn't it all been said while this little boy, only a scrap grasped, stands lost beside a sodden toy, or a tiny wagon that is used for pushing? No these are not places either, only a cover-up, a story, for nothing can remain of those irrefutable white flowers massed in summer concerns, column after column out, out. This is the kind of thing that gets in the way, all the time, wanting to go back and finding nowhere to go, as the light shower hisses down on the open petals, so white and bland, like an immense dust, covering memories over and over again. While, indoors, a much more active concern was being shown by a person attempting to carry a dead man down the narrow stairs the coffin couldn't go up. While the dead man's hands could no longer ache to reach out across the rain and take the little hand nor the bulky shoulders long for that heart-beat hug of time and its inventions, prising open a smile from a stubborn sort of silence that children get like when they're left too long.

And the dumfounded man, walking his dog, did not know there was a dead man in the house who could no longer decide to be deaf to that sound, that stopped child's voice, rising shrill, primitive, terrible, immense, clenching hard on all reason. The rain fell and the silent man, standing on the other side of the cast-iron railings, stared in at the boy with his little wagon that he used for pushing, whose cries even the stripped intrepid possible angels rehearsing judgement on the playing fields could make no sense of at all. And the next day of course everything worn so smooth with explanation you could barely notice the loss. Simply not the place you see. What after all could come to the point among so much already taken away? And the flowers, so many of them that year, so white, billowing in the summer wind, so cumbrously present.

This is what the dumfounded man sees: that the little boy who has a wagon which moves along when you push it and a toy animal sodden in the rain, is looking at the billowing white flowers for being there, when so much else could no longer be, and goes on with the dog down the embankment.

1 : 50 000
by Elizabeth James

A debut collection of witty, astringent poems which speak with intelligence, humour and poignance.

£4.99   ISBN 0951695924   32pp

VENNEL PRESS
9 Pankhurst Court, Caradon Close, London, E11 4TB

JOHN DORY

Work lovers

An induction

At interview they enjoy walking and reading.

They move away to spend more time
arriving. They still touch handles early, boast
about traffic problems,
night-clubbers like cut-outs sighted bandy-legging home,
passenger trains cancelled for overnight freight,
delayed they say, by points failures and, apparently,
a puma on the line.

Bored at home at weekends, they recreate in gardens;
later, they enthuse canteenly about cats and football,
relate relatives who stayed over before moving on.
As you know, they have photographed them.

At lunchtime they leave crumbs in iron filings
and in files on ironing.
They accept not visually any pay,
also distrusting The Unions of course.

They have already had children or will never have them.
When mothers-to-be are sacked, they privately sympathise: what
could Management do?

Breaks

Work lovers as you found them,
not servants not civil not public.
Between a sorting office and a sweat-shop
in this Age! (Turks walk out,
'riot', will not be considerate;
traffic stops.
The limping city drags: mutton
dressed as kebab.)

Between an office and a shop
orange duty-heavy cables
couple at a socket-box. Scaffolding: a house of cards
round a House of Fraser.
A chancer walks the plank,
singing: 'Working night and day,
I try to get ahead.'
A woman will not listen,
a woman does not hear,
a man hears,
a woman laughs, moves on.
' . . . I don't get ahead this way.'

Work lovers in an office
meet at a sandwich shop
also grocering greens.
He says his piece:
I believe in bull
and also little sheep.
One of each, with D-John mustard.
She says: Any starfruit today, pawpaw,
lobsterberries, or bleating-squash?

Dew Rex, king of the early morning,
early early rise. A lunch pack for midnight sandwiches.
They meet (he meets him) in Boots
the Chemist. A shopgirl assumes
he has a better half, Her Indrawers,
but here is the point-five: point blank, Man,
both, perceptibly, a handsome Item.
(They have worked it out, relaxed,
and now she has.)

You found the time
to photocopy your hands,
the matt walls of the camera a bath,
dust on the glass spinning you on its only visual splinter,
internal mail
unfolding at a wedding beginning in a multi-storey,
chuffed as car doors and then civil,
'the meeting's quorate, love,'
a little do about touch, red-eye,
and the music-stand a sapling in winter,
fuzzbox and flanger, sheet music later,
a song you know now and feed back.

VITTORIA VAUGHAN

Iphigenia

I wait for your fare well sigh,
And a contrived smile, fool
Yourself that I'll be alright.
But secretly you've tied the loose ends of your mind,
And find me slit from head to toe
By our love-making me hollow, empty, vessel.
Feed the mangle of my veins
Through your morselling machine,
Shred them lightly in between the cartilage membrane,
And bleed the juices into the ciphonous tubes.
Twist my fractured bones
Inside the coil of their jelly-cushioned joints,
Scoop my pillow muscles with their mucus covered cream
Tidily within this albumen skin.
Then nestle the yoke aside
My hall of mirrors,
And link electrodes
To charge a current through these limbs,
Shattering the panes of respectability,
Stitch my stitches with pins and needles,
Breathe my voice its weather,
And then you can leave.
Satisfied,
Glue, thread and nails might hold me in place,
Whilst I pull myself together.

YANN LOVELOCK

Walloon poetry

Walloon is the name given to the collection of Romance dialects spoken in the east of Belgium. It may be claimed as a language in the same way as Norwegian (which is also a collection of sometimes mutually incomprehensible dialects). Literature in this area dates from the 16th century but it was given a fresh boost after the creation of the Kingdom of Belgium in 1830 out of a collection of formerly independent territories divided between Flemish and Walloon speakers. It became one of the means of asserting Liege particularism in the extensive area of the former prince-bishopric and, in the 20th century, there was a poetic renaissance like that in Scots at about the same time.

A certain similarity in literary history is one reason for translating some of these poems into Scots. Another is the similarity between the reaction of a French speaker on his first encounter with Walloon and an English speaker confronting Scots. The familiar and unfamiliar are inextricably mixed, where half the time the unfamiliar is really the known in unaccustomed clothing. A third reason has to do with Hugh MacDiarmid's belief that Scots should be used for saying things impossible in the language of the majority culture. I chose the two poems for adaptation into Scots with this particularly in mind.

Remacle's 'Voyedje' has lyric qualities reminiscent of the tradition deriving from Burns. The homely matter of Grafe's 'Flibotes' recommended it for this treatment, but also the colloquial speech wedded to such a strange approach to the subject. Raymond Queneau learned the poem by heart and used to confound Parisian friends by quoting it to them. Maquet, on the other hand, is interested purely in the odd logic of the situation he describes. For this, perhaps, English is better suited.

ALBERT MAQUET (b. 1922)

From **In the Pupil's Mirror**

Without his noticing –
like a dream which leaves a stain –
in the end the shadow reached
the middle of his face.

He tried to rouse himself,
to tumble his malaise,
but his body was crumbling
like chalk into dust.

Then the shadow lay out-
stretched where he slackened
and when the light faded
they saw he was missing.

Sins qu'i s'ènn' ye aporcû –
Come on sondje qui lêt 'ne tètche –
L'ombe al fin l'aveût-st-acsû
A mitan dè vizèdje.

I saya di s'dispièrter
Po tchèssi s'må evôye.
Mins s'cwér trûléve tot costé
Come dèl poûssire di crôye.

Adon, l'ombe i s'sitanda
Tot wice qu'i s'dil kéve
Et cwand l'loumîre distinda
On vèya qu'i m kéve.

Note: Published in the collection *Djeû d'Apèles* (1947)

ROBERT GRAFE (1896–1968)

Ravels

The flitterbat keeks an' it lauchs –
mune's oot, it kens reavers are scairt.

Fer doun aneath the caister wa'
there's gowd fu' o' barrels an' a'.

Ane day oot after woodcock
the auld gillie dround in a bog.

We havena seen yon vagabones
sin he war eaten o' the wolves.

Hizzie leanin' at the winnock,
dae ye hear the cushie peughle?

Under the claith o' the pool's spate
blaws the gowan gars men forget.

Flibotes

Li tchawe-soris rèy dè saveûr
Qui l' leune a fêt sogne ås voleûrs.

I-n-a-st-ine bôme dizos l' tchèstê
Wice qu'i-n-a d' l'or plin dès tonês.

On djoû qu'i tchèssîve as bègasses,
Li vî gar nèya-st-è marasse.

On n'a pus vèyou l' rôbaleû,
C'èst qu'il a stu magnî dès leûs.

Djon.ne fèye à l' fignèsse aspoyève,
Oyez-v' li monså qui rôkèye?

Dizos l'tcûle di l'êwe dè vèvî,
Florih li fleûr qui fêt roŭi

Note: First magazine publication 1951, frequently anthologised thereafter.

LOUIS REMACLE (b. 1910)

Farin' Oot

I ligged by you, sae neigh, sae neigh,
Ye'd lips fe nouther lauch ne leid;
An' sin ye kenned weel whaur I ligged
Your lids stayed shut an I war deid.

The yird ca'd me ayont the roofs
Wi' flowers o' white i' blaewort lift:
I gaed my lane intil the spring
A' saftly for ye'd see me shift.

Ye didna ken my face nae mair
Sin syne your een had opit wide:
I'd ganged my gait owre fer, owre fer
For speirin' happiness to bide.

Voyèdje

Dj'èsteû dré vos, tot près, tot pres.
Vos d'morîz sins rîre nè djâzer;
èt v' savîz si bin la k' dj'èsteû
ku v' lèyîz vos doûs-ûs sèrés.

Mès l' têre mu houkéve oute dès teûts,
tote blanke du fleûrs duzos l' bleû cî:
dj'ènn'a nn'alé, avâ l' prétins,
tot doûcemint, sins k' vos l' vèhayîz.

Et v'la k'vos n' m'av ruc'nohou
cwand ku v's-av rudrouvi les-us:
dj'esteu evoye si lon, si lon,
ku m'bounheur nu m'aveut nin su . . .

Note: Published in the collection *A Tcheste d'Poussire* (1946)

BERTOLT BRECHT
translated by J. M. Andrews

Wheel-change

I wait at the side of the road;
The driver changes the wheel.
I don't want to be where I came from.
I don't want to be where I'm going.
So why can't I wait
For the wheel-change?

KATHLEEN McPHILEMY

Poetry in Scots: a View from the Outside

Many years ago I was living in Edinburgh and engaged in research in, among other things, the later English poetry of Hugh MacDiarmid. Inevitably, I was aware of the Scottish language issue and discussion of the merits of writing in Scots. However, it was only when I happened to attend a poetry reading in Scots given by the poet W. N. Herbert at the Museum of Modern Art in Oxford, that my interest in these matters was rekindled.

The energy of this writer and his commitment to a language which almost no-one understands raised many questions in my mind about the motivations and justifications for writing in Scots. The attempts to answer these questions led to further questions about the nature of the activity of writing poetry in any language. If we are prepared to entertain contemporary poetry in Scots we are forced to consider more closely our own unexamined assumptions about writing, mother tongue and translation.

At this point, it is necessary to draw some distinctions between different kinds of poetry in Scots current at the moment, at least so far as I have perceived them. Apart from contributions to various magazines, the two volumes on which I base most of my arguments are *The New Makars*, ed. Tom Hubbard (Mercat Press: Edinburgh, 1991), and *Sharawaggi* by Robert Crawford and W. N. Herbert (Polygon: Edinburgh, 1990). These two authors are also represented in the first anthology. It is clear from *The New Makars* that Herbert and Crawford represent one extreme of a wide spectrum of Scottish writing. At the other extreme, we find a number of contemporary or fairly contemporary examples of the kailyard verse abominated by MacDiarmid. There are also many different varieties of Scots, from Shetlandic, which I assume to be fairly closely based on a living spoken dialect, to what I would call English with a Scottish accent as, say, in the contributions of Alan Bold. Then, in the tradition of MacDiarmid, there are poems in synthetic or dictionary Scots, a made-up language whose 'makars' seem to recognise no bounds in what is allowable or may be included.

None of the writers exclude English from their poems. Of course, much of the lexis of Scots is close to what we might call standard English and often spellings indicate differences of pronunciation which do not vary from R.P. any more than those found in Yorkshire or Cornwall. But sometimes the movement from Scots to English and back again has a disjointed quality which suggests that the poet may not be entirely comfortable in his chosen medium.

There is a difference between this neither one thing nor the other approach and that of the poets who are writing so confidently in Scots that they feel able to include English, words from other languages, exotic and technical vocabulary as well as their neologisms. This delight in the quiddities of all languages is part of their inheritance from MacDiarmid and it is indulged with panache, with convincing but bewildering effrontery.

Indeed, the first effect of all these texts in Scots is to bewilder, not least because of the mechanics of presentation. There appears to be no standardisation of spelling: sometimes it is traditional, sometimes it is a phonetic approximation concocted by the poet. Why, in the same poem, do we find 'And' and 'an' as well as 'in' and 'i'? Why do some poets write 'fae' and some 'frae'? Do these differences indicate regional variations, do they follow rules of usage not apparent to the outsider, or are they attempts by the poets as individuals to score their poems for reading aloud? It would seem extremely important for the reader to be helped as much as possible to realise how the poems sound, but these inconsistencies together with the clash between English and Scots orthographies make it very difficult to 'hear' the texts.

Then there is the matter of glossaries and translations. In *The New Makars* neither the editor nor the poets seem to have decided whether or not this is a language which will be understood by the majority of readers. Consequently, the glossary is grossly inadequate. Time after time, I have looked for a word to find it missing while another word with a much more obvious translation will be given. The editor should either have dispensed with the glossary altogether and insisted on sending readers to the dictionary, or have provided a much more substantial glossary. However, if you expect your readers to buy or have access to a Scots dictionary you are probably restricting your readership to academics and those who are already involved with Scots. This would seem to be an inward-looking and undesirable consequence. Of course, the problem is partly the root uncertainty as to whether or not this is a foreign language. If it were, we could expect either to learn the language or to rely on translation. As it is, most people, especially those who are Scottish and have a greater or lesser residual knowledge of Scots, will not expect to have to learn the language. Consequently, since they are not offered a translation they have to make their own, often based on the uncertainty of guesswork. In *Sharawaggi*, recognising these difficulties, Crawford and

Herbert offer glossaries and translations which are disingenuous and to which I shall return.

The reader of poetry, as of anything else, has a need to evaluate it, and it is particularly difficult to evaluate these poems in Scots. In some respects, the problem is the same as that of evaluating poetry in translation. It is hard to tell if what you admire has been imported into the poem by the translator or, conversely, if the translator's ineptitude has betrayed the quality of the poem. Thus we may fail to appreciate a poem in Scots because of our own inadequate translation. On the other hand we may be beguiled by the novelty of the lexis into overvaluing the poem which employs it. Of course a poem is the words which compose it, but if the sentiments or meaning are banal, it cannot be redeemed by the vocabulary, however fresh and unfamiliar. Sometimes it is the form which lacks energy.

The gangrel Bodie

She was aye that sleekit
Ye niver kent
Whaur she hid come fae,
Whaur she wis bent.
Like a tod in the mirk
That smools through the haar,
She wis here an awa
An ye didnae ken whaur.

(Sheila Douglas)

This is not unpleasing and lines 5 and 6 are more than that, but there does not seem to be much point to it. It is conventional in its use of rhyme and metre (as are many of the poems in the anthology). There is nothing intrinsically wrong with traditional forms, but their frequent recurrence as ballads, lyrics, and even music hall style verse reflect an unertainty of purpose. In what sense are these 'new' makars? It can't be based on the criterion of age, as several of those included are old, near contemporaries of the founders of the Scottish Renaissance. Nor do they apparently have to be innovators, since many of the poets seem to be doing little more than recycling Scots vocabulary in traditional ways. They run a danger of falling into the 'heritage' trap, like the tin miners in Cornwall who work not to extract tin, but to amuse the tourists. And if the desire to amuse the tourists is carried too far, there is a risk of self-caricature, of using Scots to confirm stereotypes in a terrible jokiness which devalues the language and its people. This was something which worried me about, for instance, the contributions from Janet Paisley:

Ah'm shy. Aye, ah am. Canny look naebody in the eye.
Ah've seen me go in a shoap an jist hoap naebody wid talk tae me.
Things that happen, likesae – yer oot fur a walk
an some bloke whits never even spoke afore goes by
an he's givin ye the eye. See me, ah jist want tae die.
Ah go rid tae the roots o ma hair. Weel it's no fair, is it.

(from 'Sharleen: Ah'm Shy')

Although entertaining and although they have a feel for authentic speech rhythms, such poems give the impression of the poet 'doing a turn', making fun of the poorly-educated working class girls who are her subjects. This anthropological flavour extends to other poems in the anthology such as Ken Morrice's 'Domiciliary Visit' or the rather smug ballad-style poems by Alan Bold.

Many of the poets are writing with a political motivation. It is noticeable from the biographical section how many have been involved in Scottish nationalist politics or in the active promotion of Scottish language and culture. However, writing in Scots because of political conviction may not be enough to produce an energised poetry. Portrayals of the horrendous conditions of coal-mines, indictments of advertising, condemnations of inequality are no more than social commentary if the indignation which has fired emotion has not also fired the language. When this does happen, we get successful poetry, as, I think, in very different ways, the extracts from Bill Sutherland's 'Clydesdale Lad' and Kate Armstrong's 'Graffito' show.

In Sutherland's poem, or in the extract given here, he succeeds in his stated aim of 'conveying the spirit of his working class background from its jokes to its deepest aspirations and loves'. Although he uses traditional form and rhyme the energy of his language is such that his poetry is strengthened not stultified:

An though you think he's big an braw,
him in his burton suit an aw,
Ah've heard he disnae gie hie-haw –
but don't come running back tae me.

Kate Armstrong's poem, without the restraining devices of regular rhyme or verse pattern, careers along with a crazy, drunken energy which perhaps is an identifiable characteristic of Scottish poetry and which again presents difficulties for those accustomed to the more staid and rational behaviour of most English poetry:

Stanes are fer chuckin; stanes are aye tae haund.
Wee antrin syllables fund thir yird
lanesome. Ae day, a scriff o wind
skelpit them intae a spray-can, intae life.
Nae man casts concrete owre me.

This poem seems to be a plea for a Scots that is particular, vigorous, indigenous, from the streets, but at the same time open to the cross-fertilisation of other languages and cultures: ' . . . the leid ye screive dunts mine, mine yers, / twa cairdboats aye rowin the yae sea.' Here, perhaps, is the ideal aimed for and that which is hearkened back to in evocations of pre-Union independence. Scottish culture is envisioned as strong and individual but open to the cultures of Europe and the world.

It may be this desire to be in touch with other languages and literatures which accounts for the extraordinarily high numbers of translations in *The New Makars*. By my reckoning, up to a fifth of the poems are translations, free versions or otherwise derivative from works of literature in other languages. One could put forward a number of suggestions why this might be so. The most unkind might be that some of these translators have nothing of their own to write and so are forced to plunder other literature. But perhaps we should remember the huge amount of translating and Englishing done by Chaucer, Wyatt, Surrey and others which provided much of the foundations for modern English literature. Perhaps Scots needs this enrichment from external literatures, this grafting on of foreign stock. However, I cannot view translating *MacBeth* into Scots as a very fruitful activity. It seems closer to *Winnie-the-Pooh* in Latin than any serious poetic endeavour.

There are other translations from familiar European sources: Villon, Dante, Heine, etc. A distinction can be drawn between these and translations from more contemporary poets such as Vallejo, Montale, Ernesto Cardenal and Erich Fried, where translation is both an entry into and a building up of the international community of poetry. Translation from another language directly into Scots is also an assertion that other poetries need not be mediated through English. It may even be claimed that Scots is in some cases a more appropriate medium. This is argued by Edwin Morgan in translating Mayakovsky: 'There is in Scottish poetry (e.g. Dunbar, Burns and MacDiarmid) a vein of fantastic satire that seems to me to accommodate Mayakovsky more readily than anything in English verse'.[1] Even if this is true, however, English cannot be entirely eliminated from the process. It is interesting that in Morgan's introduction all the quotations from Mayakovsky are given in English. And, of course, the book contains a considerable glossary which is an acknowledgement that English must enter into the process of the reader's apprehension. There is no doubt that the Mayakovsky which appears in Scots is different from the 'English' Mayakovsky, as can be seen from the most cursory comparison of Morgan's *Wi the Haill Voice* with, for instance, George Reavey's *At the Top of My Voice*.[2] The English version is much more obviously a translation, its respect for the original giving it a churchy stiltedness. Morgan, on the other hand, takes the poem over for Scotland, using Scottish references to assimilate it: 'auld Willy Lochheid / gies my hame nae plenishin' (an allusion to a posh Glasgow furniture store). At the same time, by using Scots, the under-language, a language not previously considered fit for print, he does achieve a feeling of revolution, of the upsurge of the people, which seems appropriate to Mayakovsky.

So we return to the political aspect of writing in Scots. All these poets are held together by their decision to write in Scots and this is a political decision. Whether they are avowed Scottish nationalists or whether they eschew party politics, their poems are acts of subversion. They contradict received notions of acceptable poetic diction, and like the new Afro-Caribbean or Creole writing or contemporary writing in Scottish or Irish Gaelic, they assert cultures and traditions which have been overwhelmed by the predominance of English. It is perhaps the feeling of solidarity with other oppressed cultures that accounts for the surprisingly high number of translations from unfamiliar minority and non-European languages like Basque, Tamil and Vietnamese.

The New Makars is ultimately an unsatisfactory anthology which contains hints of what could have been a much more exciting book. *Sharawaggi*, by Robert Crawford and W. N. Herbert, tail-enders in the first collection, offers a 'new' with more substance and meaning. These poets write with enormous self-consciousness, willingly embracing the difficulties and contradictions of the medium they have chosen. They bring to their work a wide knowledge of world literatures as well as the knowingness of a post-modern critical training. Over their writing broods the still unassimilated presence of MacDiarmid.

This seems to me to be a poetry led by language, where the poets accept the problems and constraints of writing in Scots because the dictionaries and the dialects bring them to new possibilities. The process of writing seems to become a reversal of conventional practice, with the words which the poet has discovered in the dictionary pressing him into service, instead of the poet harnessing the language for the realisation of his vision.

This preoccupation with language in general and the Scots language in particular results in an opaque poetry where the density of the words obscures any underlying experience, if, indeed, we have any reason to expect such a thing. We are constantly reminded that poems operate in the world of words and that they need not refer to 'reality'. In a poem like 'Burns Ayont Auld Reekie' the extraordinary exuberance of imagery should not be regarded as surreal, a revelation of the unconscious, but rather as an exhibition of possibilities in language which are nonsensical in the real world. On the other hand Herbert seems in his poetry to believe that the language can unlock realities of mind, the id, unconscious or whatever. Certainly, some of his poems have a disturbing power not common in English, and convey emotion or mixtures of emotion which we recognise but might not have owned to, as for instance in 'Grout and Pamisample':

Eh saw inside ootfrae thi sile o ma mind
a billatory rise, aa bowdens in
thi gosky gress. An whaur the een
sud be, Picasso's jet in curlin daurk,
twa nichthawks did Eh see, faibil
white oan gallus luchts, an whaur
thi nostrils nichthawks, and aa
uts mooth mumbudjit wi moth:
ile-grout oan shore. Grout an pamisample.

Using Scots where the language itself confers opacity Herbert and Crawford can forgo the irony which has debilitated so much of contemporary English poetry. It is noticeable how much more exuberant and indecorous Crawford's Scots poems are than his writing in English. It may also be that the vigorous – even violent – thread in the Scottish literary tradition enables poets to write in modes they would not essay in English. But there is a difficulty with this foregrounding of language. If we are denied the possibility of external reference the poem may set out on a journey but fail to carry the reader along with it.

It is worth considering at this point the very strange game Crawford is playing in the translations which he provides for a number of these poems. In fact I would suggest that they are themselves prose poems and their disguise as translations allows him to write in a way which would be unacceptable and indeed ludicrous if presented as an English original: ' . . . [I] anxiously enquire about love. I'm unembarrassedly ready, and know my equipment . . . '. Moreover, when he translates 'randy yuppies' as 'randy young urban professionals' we realise that we are being strung along. The presentation of the poems as dual texts is a constant temptation to abandon the Scots for the apparently more accessible English. But after being dragged headlong through Crawford's minimally punctuated rush of imagery, the reader returns to the Scots, where the line-breaks and movement of the verse serve to steady the poem. The reader who perseveres will apprehend neither the Scots or English version in isolation, but his or her own amalgam of both. The willingness to persevere may fail where Crawford loses the reader's trust, where we suspect the temptations of the dictionary have resulted in self-indulgence. This happens for me with 'Room of thi Loof':

Aneath yon lither we plout-net fur thi time
That's cummin tae slee in, thi time whan we'll mak
Wurd's paddock-hair gang packlie, an loo skyre oot
Its yule-blinker fund in thi yarkins.

Beneath that yielding sky with undulating clouds, using a small stocking-shaped net and two poles, we search for the time that's coming to slip free in, when we'll make the unfledged down of words work intimately, and love shine out clearly its north star discovered in the side seams of a shoe.

These writers have accepted the description of 'Scottish baroque' with its implications of excess and decorative flourish, a style which seems to contravene conventional rules for 'good writing'. Yet, by scouring the dictionary and, I am certain, at times making words up ('imparmigination – that aspect of the intellect which finds pleasure in the baroque and manneristic'?) these poets recover the immediacy and excitement pursued differently by Pound and the Imagists. For the Imagists the goal was to recreate in words as accurately as possible a moment of experience when 'a thing outward and objective transforms itself, or darts into a thing inward and subjective'.[3] Ideally, this recording would be in terms of external observables so that it would excite the same sensations or emotions in the reader as experienced by the poet. This is, of course, a gross over-simplification but it does recall the importance of 'out there', external reality outside language. In the same way many of the Scots words which have been excavated from the dictionary act together with their translations as miniature Imagist poems. They restore to mind areas of reality we have not had names for, and, in particular, because of their specificity, areas of Scottish reality. We remark how many words reflect the climactic and seasonal peculiaritites of Scotland. For instance there are many words to describe the in-between times of dawn and twilight which are so much longer in the North. Much of the vocabulary reflects the pre-industrial past. The peat-cutter (flauchter-spad) and the hamshackled beast sit oddly with the post-romantic sensibility. Yet, as in Herbert's poem 'Bullseye', the castrated bull and emasculated language meet in the central metaphor. The history of Scotland preserved in the language strengthens the poem.

Though this poetry is anchored in various ways to reality, the manner in which the language itself seems self-generating, spawning image and metaphor independent of experience, moves towards pure aestheticism, the art object whose business is not to mean but to be. There is no logical argument against this, though personal morality and private opinion may cry out. Poetry is a mixed art; words are used to convey meaning as well as to make pictures and sounds. Pound analysed three strands in poetry: melopoeia, phanopoeia and logopoeia. Without logopoeia, the argument, there is a reduction in satisfaction. By argument, I do not mean a philosophical discourse, but the element in a poem which seeks to communicate, to articulate and share experience. It is only through a belief in shared experience and at the very least, the overlapping of our private languages that the writing of poetry let alone the act of translating it can become a possible or sensible activity.

It would be wrong to say that good poetry is always difficult, but if a poem is to extend our understanding, rather than merely confirm what we already know, effort must be involved. However there is a risk of leaving too many terms unknown. Faced with a poem in a language we don't fully understand, where there is either no reference to the external world or the reference is private, readers may feel there is not enough to sustain them and abandon their reading. Crawford and Herbert convince us that they are enormously talented, exuberant and extremely clever. But they do run the risk of writing to please themselves and a few friends and to annoy a slightly wider circle of foes. Because of the very quality and intensity of their work, however, I think they escape this charge of wilful hermeticism.

The choked opaque (baroque) texture of these poems forces us to examine our own writing practice. I don't know that it would ever be possible to write like this in English. I don't know that it is possible to write in Scots or any other variety of non-standard English unless the basic sounds and rhythms are in your blood. But I do re-examine my own aims in writing, which seem to be to make the language apparently transparent and as close as possible to the rhythms and vocabulary of the world of speech which I inhabit. I am unlikely to change my ways but I am obliged to admit that I am not so much trying to write naturally as to conceal artifice. Language can never be transparent and to act as if it were reveals a certain kind of 'take' on the world which is necessarily a limiting one. It may also be that for historical reasons successful writing in English tends to be in this mode, and that this need not be true for Scots or indeed other languages.

I would not take *The New Makars* to my desert island. On the other hand, *Sharawaggi* is something I will return to and continue to argue with. It is a very 'smart' book, a polemic and a manifesto which disguises itself in incomprehensibility. However, beyond the exasperation, it repays struggle.

* * *

Have you practis'd so long to learn to read?
Have you felt so proud to get at the meaning of poems?[4]

Notes

1 *Wi the Haill Voice: 25 poems by Vladimir Mayakovsky*, translated into Scots by Edwin Morgan (Oxford: Carcanet, 1972).
2 See *The Penguin Book of Socialist Verse*, ed. Alan Bold (Harmondsworth: Penguin, 1970).
3 'Vorticism', in *Fortnightly Review*, Vol. 96, 1914, reprinted in *Gaudier-Brzeska* (London: Faber, 1960).
4 'Song of Myself' in *Walt Whitman: The Complete Poems*, ed. Frances Murphy (Harmondsworth: Penguin, 1975), 64.

G A I R F I S H

edited by W. N. Herbert and Richard Price

CREATIVE WORK IN ALL THE LANGUAGES OF SCOTLAND

THE RADICAL REAPPRAISAL OF SCOTTISH CULTURE

COHESIVE COLLECTIONS OF ESSAYS AND POETRY

DISCOVERY: Robert Burns, Darwin, John Buchan, and Frank O'Hara.

THE ANARCHY OF LIGHT: A Celebration of Neil M. Gunn

DUENDE: A DUNDEE ANTHOLOGY Douglas Dunn, Tracey Herd, Andrew Fox, Sean O'Brien, Anne Stevenson

Gairfish poets include: Meg Bateman, John Burnside, Margaret Gillies Brown, Stewart Conn, James Aitchison, Edwin Morgan, Robert Crawford, Aonghas Macneacail, John Glenday, David Kinloch, Alan Riach, and Donny O'Rourke.

Each volume £3.50. Available at all good bookshops or direct from the publisher:

GAIRFISH, 34 Gillies Place, Broughty Ferry, Dundee.

PETER McCAREY

The Tum-ti-tum Epithet

> Slowly along the munching English lane,
> Like cows to the old shrine, until you lose
> Track of your dragging pain.

That should be 'mulching', shouldn't it? (Did nobody proofread *Robert Lowell's Poems: A Selection*, ed. Jonathan Raban?) though the dragging pain and big beasts might hint at anthropophagy rather than bacteriophages.

Looking up the page from 'Our Lady of Walsingham' to 'The Holy Innocents' I notice a 'clinkered hill' up which the year lumbers with losses. Shouldn't that be 'clinkered hull'? . . . No. But I'm on my guard now. Next is the corpse in 'The Quaker Graveyard in Nantucket', 'its heel-bent deity' surely, surely that should be 'hell-bent'? And 'the coiled, hurdling muscles of his thighs'? Could it be 'curdling muscles'? Makes just a bit more sense to me. Maybe 'eel-bent deity'; I'll let anything pass after the 'ale-wife run' of the first poem.

A decent edition wouldn't solve the problem, which is: that Lowell once said he hoped people would read his work and say 'that was one heck of a poet' or something of the sort (sorry, can't find the reference). He is one heck of a poet. And he's always trying hard to stay one, putting an adjectival spin on nouns that would otherwise have been plainer. He polishes his work till the reader can see his face in it. Lowell's.

What is it about adjectives? Their syntactic redundancy (take them all away and the sentences still work), their prosthetic virtues (for dragging rhythms), the fact that they know their place and rarely come wide. All this was a boon to bards and other oral improvisers, giving poet and audience a moment's rest: the berry-brown gown or, south and east, the rosy-fingered dawn. People who *read* poetry, though, take their own time off. While the adjective still serves as a rhythmic and syntactic rest, it often takes a lot of semantic weight, or strain. Like when Ezra Pound alludes (in Greek) to the rosy-fingered dawn, telling us to think of Homer before breakfast, or when Lowell hits us with the above examples.

Fear not, this isn't a grand unified theory of epithets. It's just interesting to see that the disconcerting effect of Lowell's bravura is what language poets contrive by other means. Astounding adjective and noun pairs may be produced by the Poet of Genius ('the gun-blue swingle' or whatever you like); they may also be produced by the OULIPO S+7 method ('S+7 veut dire simplement qu'on remplace tous les substantifs d'un texte par le septieme qui le suit dans un lexique donné'). This nicely sabotages the ego as the source of all poetry. It leads the unwary to conclude that the text, however produced, is all we should look at. And that's a load of balls. I don't like feeling that a poet I'm reading is spending too much effort on impressing me; but better that than a nihilistic purveyor of text and nothing but the text (Ashbery). I've more sympathy for some of the language poets, but in the end 'change the language' is not what it's about. A quick look at three poets who could tell them.

> Ah how bright the mantel
> Brass shines over me.
> Black-lead at my elbow,
> Pipe-clay at my feet.
> (W. S. Graham)

This whole business of epithets intervenes at a late (prolonged and tedious) stage of the poem's formation, when the plasma settles down into little nuclear families and the charges get distributed. 'Mantel' gives the brass an ingot shape, 'black-' combines with lead to form a shining compound, 'pipe-' reacts with 'clay' as candour, the honest ornament. There isn't an adjective in sight. The colours are all substantive. Remove them and the sentences collapse, the hearth with them.

How can adjectives be used in an essential way? Let's see if that's a fair question. Even in Graham's weird first collection, the adjectives aren't responsible for much of the disorientation: true there are bloodshot pennies, myrtle gospels and a nettle forefinger, but there are also limestone viaducts, a boatless sea, blushing joy and a gentle queen, all as reassuring as the conventional sentence structure. Adjectives are weak parts of speech and Graham doesn't overload them. Indeed, until 'The Nightfishing' he's a bit too easy on them. And while 'sheerhulk', 'girlflowering', 'mastertask' and the other Anglosaxoid shunts are looking for integrity, the epithets – high, bright, new, black, white, blue, green, dry, terrible, dead, drowned – are trying to forge the elements that he struck in the later 'Malcolm Mooney's Land'. Sleekit metaphor, not fair at all; it's just a way of saying I don't completely trust his words until then. And anyway, where's the law against putting a semantic load on a weak part of speech? It isn't a matter of law, but discretion. Lowell bends everything to his purpose – that's his way. Graham tries to devine the language's purpose and go its way.

> Outside the tent endless
> Drifting hummock crests.
> Words drifting on words.
> The real unabstract snow.
>   (end of 'Malcolm Mooney's Land')

> 'It must be abstract'
>   (Wallace Stevens)

Some critics like to lay down the law: never mind old plods like John Bayley. Look at Randall Jarrell, telling us bad poetry is not good and abstract poetry is not poetry (the latter a propos of Wallace Stevens, whose earlier work he praises highly). Well (A) most poetry is bad: it's a mug's game, and (B) the rest can be as it pleases: 'The real unabstract snow' is utter abstraction, lyophilised.

Each Stevens poem is an abstraction, an architectural model on computer. The components can be either images or ideas, but the plan's the thing.

> Poetry is the supreme fiction, madame.
> Take the moral law and make a nave of it.
> And from the nave build haunted heaven. Thus,

thankyou. Epithets. There are two distinctive tribes in Stevens, the colours and the quizzicals. The colours are primary, and lights rather than pigments (the reverse is true of Graham), slanting in and suffusing the things – golden floor, red bird, pool of pink, bright chromes, colored purple, white moonlight, green shade – to look no further than the first twenty pages of the collected poems. And while the colour epithets show, the quizzicals see (light source and viewpoint respectively, in the computer image). 'The Doctor of Geneva' has a swatch of them, as the good doctor is seen reacting to a new location: lacustrine man, multifarious heavens, simmering mind, unburgherly apocalypse. Stevens quickly escapes anything as crass as a scanning of his epithets, though the exercise confirms that he isn't content with making his poems: in his tremendous ambition that poetry succeed religion, he lets there be light on them with his 'purple' adjectives, and he doubts and believes in them with his quirky epithets.

I had in mind a further manic leap, to Mandelstam, but I'm running out of steam. If Anglosax was W. S. Graham's handicap, then Greek (and Homeric epithets) was Mandelstam's. Still, it's nice to see how in the poem to JSB he sets up 'O ratiocinatory Bach' (or 'Most reasonable, judicious Bach') to increase the thrill of the punchline, with Bach 'exulting like Isaiah', and in 'I washed in the courtyard at night', how the epithet 'coarse' applied to stars prepares for 'In the rain-butt a star melts like salt'. As he progresses, though, I can't easily distinguish what he's planned from what the language serves him. There are, for me, terrible difficulties in 'The Slate Ode' because although Mandelstam's (anybody's) rhyme is exogamy that breaks the dominion of familiar etymological association, Mandelstam seems to reach far into the past of his words as well, where family is not familiar at all. Thus a lot of his weird findings, that have neither rhyme nor reason in a foreign language like English, turn out to have semantic precedents at home.

> Flint meets water and ring joins horseshoe;
> On the soft shale of the clouds
> A milky slate-grey sketch is drawn.
>> (from *Osin Mandeistam: Fifty Poems*, translated by Bernard Meares, with an introduction by Joseph Brodsky (New York, Persea Books, 1977) sadly out of print)

Now 'persten' (signet ring) is cognate with 'perst' (breast) (the ring being a nipple substitute, apparently) that goes with the 'milk slate sketch' of the following line. And 'kremen' (flint) is cognate with 'shram' (scratch or scar), so that when at the end he writes:

> I want to place my fingers
> In the flinty path from the older song
> As in a lesion . . .

the thing begins to make sense. Begins to. Enough.

I am now in a position to conclude both that there are at least four ways of skinning a cat, and that that conclusion gets me no nearer the rough taxonomy I was out to establish. I don't think, anyway, that taxonomy would have shed any light on the light shed by certain poems, or that that would have been useful or possible. Escape. Save. Quit.

ALAN RIACH

Tradition and the New Alliance: Scotland and the Caribbean

1. Colonising Scotland

When the Head of the Maori Studies Department at the University of Waikato ascertained that I had come from Scotland, he told me with pleasure that he had, in his time, visited the Edinburgh International Festival and witnessed the Edinburgh Military Tattoo. He said that he could not understand how any Scot could fail to take pride in such a splendid display of the singular culture of Scotland.

I could say nothing at the time but I was thinking of Hugh MacDiarmid's remark apropos the Edinburgh Military Tattoo. He called it a disgraceful spectacle by an army of occupation upon a nation of sheep.[1]

And yet the Head of the Maori Studies Department was right. The spectacle *does* 'display' a very singular aspect of Scotland's colonial culture. And it does so proudly, with a remarkable and characteristic lack of irony.

2. Departures

My original intention with this paper was to work through a number of historical instances where Scotland and the Caribbean could be seen in reciprocal contact.[2] I outlined the plan I thought I might adopt in my abstract, and I began to think about ways in which theoretical understanding of traditions and precedents worked with unique historical instances in terms of both Caribbean and Scottish literature.

Scottish poets were among the earliest to describe the Caribbean in verse, working, paradoxically, in a predominantly English pastoral tradition. The work of James Grainger and James Montgomery, for example, belongs to the literary tradtion of the Caribbean, but it also must be understood in relation to eighteenth-century conventions of pastoral. While these conventions have been formulated in the context of the English literary tradition, they were brought about by Scots writers such as Ramsay and Thomson. Their literary distinction is found in the peculiar eighteenth-century Scottish practice of inhabiting English models.

Scottish literature has continued to exert a singular influence in the Caribbean, with Claude McKay's deliberate emulation of Burns, Edward Kamau Brathwaite's explicit recognition of the Scots linguistic component in Creole and 'nation language' and most significantly in Wilson Harris's novel *Black Marsden*, which is 'set' in Scotland.

This paper details some of the historical and theoretical complexities raised by these questions, considers the textual significance of Scots forms working in the Caribbean literary imagination, and proposes an alliance between Scottish and Caribbean literature, or to re-fashion the terms, between the colonies abroad and the 'home-colonies'.

To describe the cultural challenge of the Caribbean, Michael Gilkes offered the provocative term 'Creative Schizophrenia'. This paper argues that the term is equally provocative and equally useful with reference to modern Scottish literature, and that our understanding and reading of 'post-colonial' literatures is reciprocal with a more incisive understanding and reading of the different components of 'English literature'.

But the more I considered the matter the less satisfactory this approach seemed, so I decided to defer any attempt at a coherent and concluded paper dealing with those matters described – such as the transference of eighteenth century pastoral traditions across or through Scottish, English and Caribbean models.

If the route I finally chose seems circuitous or if I should deviate up a few blind alleys or one-way streets, then perhaps we might keep in mind the encouraging maxim from *Beyond Good and Evil* where Nietzsche tells us that deviations, non-sequiturs, digressions and rambling enquiries that seem to go nowhere are all signs of health: anything absolute belongs in the realm of the pathological.

3. Transgressions

In *The Empire Writes Back*, Bill Ashcroft, Gareth Griffiths and Helen Tiffin discuss the work of Max Dorsinville with regard to the relation between dominated and dominating societies, hierarchies of oppression and the social politics of cultural change, both within and between societies. Dorsinville's model accounts for productions of literary and cultural minorities within one country or area, such as the contemporary hierarchy of domination involved in the sequence Australian Aboriginal/white Australian/British and English literatures, or the historical hierarchy of colonial and postcolonial literature in the United States, through the eighteenth, nineteenth and twentieth centuries.

> A model such as Dorsinville's also makes less problematical the situation of Irish, Welsh and Scottish literatures in relation to the English 'mainstream'. While it is possible to argue that these societies were the first victims of English expansion, their subsequent complicity in the British imperial enterprise makes it difficult for colonised peoples outside Britain to accept their identity as post-colonial. Dorsinville's dominated-dominating model forcefully stresses linguistic and cultural imposition, and enables an interpretation of British literary history as a process of hierarchical interchange in internal and external group relationships.[3]

This begs a number of important questions. *For whom* does Dorsinville's model make the situation become 'less problematical'? *In what sense* is English to be understood as the 'mainstream' (even if that word comes with inverted commas)? And is the condition of Irish, Welsh, and Scottish literatures really a problem 'for colonised peoples outside Britain'? The crucial central sentence in the paragraph just quoted surely deserves to be rewritten in some way: 'While it is *necessary* to argue that these societies were the first victims of (not so much 'English expansion' as) *the project of Empire*, their subsequent complicity in that project – and their intimate relation to the dominating impetus – means that it is impossible to extricate their position fully from that project and that dominating impetus.' Yet without some attempt to fathom the autonomous energies at work in these societies, the monolith of English literature will continue to embrace or overshadow the literatures which have transgressed themselves and fallen prey to the project of Empire which 'English literature' was intended to serve.

When I think of those writers and critics with whom I have discussed similar questions and who themselves are extremely conscious of and sensitive to the hybrid nature of transgressive literatures, writers such as Wilson Harris, Edward Kamau Brathwaite and David Dabydeen, I am left in no doubt that they readily appreciate the complex nature and historically ambivalent status of the literature of what we might call the 'home-colonies'. And in a lecture given at the University of Cambridge in November 1990, Wilson Harris had this to say:

> There are frontiers and border lines which one might sense have been crossed in ways that are not always easily recognised. I would like to note here that when one speaks of *English* literature, one tends to forget that there are traditions which nourish English literature which come out

Scotland, out of Wales, and out of Ireland. There is a complicated reality here. Michael Gilkes, in an excellent essay, spoke of 'Creative Schizophrenia'. There is a *creative* potential in this splitting, as well as entrenched blindnesses. Think of the layers of potential creativity in Scotland. For example, there is a Celtic imagination there and there is a rich and complex layering of inheritance. In language, there is Gaelic, there is Scots and there is English. Hugh MacDiarmid tried to bring that complex creativity back, to bring all the layers into play, and achieved a great deal. The matter of 'Creative Schizophrenia' which Michael Gilkes identifies with the Caribbean, then, is pertinent in many parts of the world today. Michael Gilkes's understanding of the Caribbean shows how we might begin to have links and bridges and connections across all the traditional frontiers. All of this is pertinent to the arts of the imagination wherever they are practised.[4]

4. Outposts and Origins

Wherever they are practised?

Even in the furthest outposts of Empire – and here I include the university where I work, in New Zealand, the arts of the imagination are evolving. These are, naturally enough, places where Empire-building continues in an inescapably ironic (and perhaps even comic) way.

It seems to me evident that the status of what is awkwardly called 'post-colonial literature' is problematic in exactly the same way as the status of 'Scottish literature'. And if the problems involve very tangible questions of national, cultural and linguistic identity they also are liable to be considered in greater depth and at greater length within the academy than in any other place. Because it is within the academy that such literatures are defined for the convenience of the structures of curricula.[5]

Much of the problem with English Studies in universities derives from the piecemeal way in which cross cultural studies have developed within the discipline. As Mark Williams has argued, the development of 'Commonwealth' literature as a recognised area within English Studies was encouraged in the first place as much by imperial nostalgia and the academic interest for new territories as by disinterested attention to a very disparate body of new writing.

The term which has come to replace 'Commonwealth literature', 'Post-colonial literature', announces its determination directly to confront the political and cultural cruxes of post-colonial experience, yet if it is politically less embarrassing it is also an attempt to group together for teaching purposes all those parts of the English-speaking world other than the United States and the British Isles. Its existence is predicated on the Structural needs of English

Studies in the universities. After all, it is traditional, in universities, to teach literature according to nationalities, or historical periods, or thematically, or according to genre. It is therefore *appropriate* that there is no single term for that area to which the writing of Wilson Harris might be said to belong. There is a Centre for Research in the New Literatures in English, and there are courses on Commonwealth or Post-colonial literature – but not one of these terms is accurate to all the kinds of literature each seeks to encompass.

What this inaccuracy derives from is the failure to address the problem underlying the term *'English literature'*: that is, the fact that it is possible to identify the English language with the English nation only at the cost of ignoring a vast amount of political fact. At this point, I have to declare a personal interest. In the late 1980s, Aberdeen University Press (which is, ironically enough, a member of 'the Pergamon group' and therefore part of the Robert Maxwell empire) produced a four-volume *History of Scottish literature*.[6] As a consequence, it is now possible, almost for the first time, for most literate Scots to have some access to an account of their literature. Such an account was certainly not available for Robert Burns in the eighteenth century or even for Hugh MacDiarmid in the present century.

Of course, literary history was an eighteenth-century invention, along with the Encyclopedias and the Dictionaries. It is less often noted that English literature itself was an eighteenth-century Scottish invention and that its earliest moments are the record of a remarkable instance of colonialist subjugation, a few years after the disastrous massacre of Jacobite forces at Culloden, in 1746. Adam Smith in 1751 and Hugh Blair in 1762 were the first university lecturers teaching 'English literature', and they were working in Scotland. They set about enabling provincial Scots to engage with the culture of England on their own culture's ground. Blair was in effect the first Professor of English literature, and became such in Edinburgh. This took place less than half a century after the union of the parliaments of Scotland and England – a union which marked the abrogation of Scots political autonomy. And that itself took place scarcely one hundred years after the union of the crowns of Scotland and England, when, on the death of Queen Elizabeth the First, James the Sixth of Scotland became James the First of Great Britain – the central moment of transition from the Elizabethan to the Jacobean Renaissance, the 'crux', if I might so put it, of the 'torso' of 'English Studies'.[7]

In other words, the original moments of the discipline known as English were locked into a colonial political situation and were empowered by a colonial ideology.

The Aberdeen University Press *History of Scottish Literature* is predicated on a desire to reverse a bureaucratic whitening of language and culture, yet, paradoxically, it derives from the great projects of empire. It affirms authoritative values at the same time as it questions them. It canonizes the texts of Scottish literature while it attempts to refute the marginal status of those texts in the English literary canon.

In a sense, therefore, the Scottish condition is paradigmatically colonial. What the Scots write is not what they read. Everything is dispersed; there is no ready-made tradition. As Peter McCarey has said, few Scottish writers hit the ground running and many just hit the ground. The winners make literature and the rest make history, leaf-mould for later growth. Each writer has to find his or her own traditions – in history, in oral tradition or elsewhere. For this reason cultural and historical backgrounds are especially important in the study of Scottish literature – much more so than the establishment of canonical texts. This calls for an approach to literary studies in general which inevitably will be uncomfortable, to say the least, with a discipline which assumes there is a single central line or a 'mainstream' of major literary works running from Chaucer by way of Shakespeare and Milton to the Romantics and on, retaining a recognisable continuity. (F. R. Leavis himself was profoundly sceptical about extending that continuity beyond D. H. Lawrence.) Such an approach to literary studies in general must be equally sceptical of a canonical tradition which runs in a purely linear chronology from Henryson and Dunbar through Burns and Scott to MacDiarmid and our contemporaries.

5. Specifics

At this point I think I might return, however briefly, to my abstract, where I mention the work of James Grainger and James Montgomery. These poets were writing at the beginning of the Caribbean literary tradition and as such you will find their work in *The Penguin Book of Caribbean Verse* in the appropriate place.

Let me quote a passage from James Grainger's 'The Sugar-Cane':

> Then earthquakes, nature's agonising pangs,
> Oft shake the astonied isles: the solfaterre
> Or sends forth thick, blue, suffocating steams;
> Or shoots to temporary flame. A din,
> Wild, thro' the mountain's quivering rocky caves,
> Like the dread Crash of tumbling planets, roars.
> When tremble thus the pillars of the globe,

Like the tall coco by the fierce North blown;
Can the poor, brittle tenements of man
Withstand the dread convulsion? Their dear homes,
(Which shaking, tottering, crashing, bursting, fall)
The boldest fly; and, on the open plain
Appal'd, in agony the moment wait,
When, with disrupture vast, the waving earth
Shall whelm them in her sea-disgorging womb.[8]

And also from James Montgomery's 'The West Indies':

Dreadful as hurricanes, athwart the main
Rush'd the fell legions of invading Spain;
With fraud and force, with false and fatal breath,
(Submission bondage, and resistance death,)
They swept the isles. In vain the simple race
Kneel'd to the iron sceptre of their grace,
Or with weak arms their fiery vengeance braved;
They came, they saw, they conquer'd, they enslaved,
And they destroy'd; – the generous heart they broke,
They crush'd the timid neck beneath the yoke;
Where'er to battle march'd their grim array,
The sword of conquest plough'd resistless way;
Where'er from cruel toil they sought repose,
Around, the fires of devastation rose.
The Indian, as he turn'd his head in flight,
Beheld his cottage flaming through the night,
And, midst the shricks of murder on the wind,
Heard the mute blood-hound's death-step close behind.[9]

All I would like to suggest here is that strictly in terms of traditions it would be a fascinating study to examine the kind of 'creative schizophrenia' which links these poets, on the one hand, through a tradition of Caribbean writing to the rhetorical magniloquence of Derek Walcott, and, on the other hand, back and across to their contemporary Anglo-Scot, James Thomson, author of *The Seasons*, and indeed to the pastoral poetry of Robert Burns.

In other words, the essential struggle between articulation and position is singularly pertinent here, in terms of a peculiar rhetorical structure slipping between two modes of definition. It is true that these modes of definition are formed in similar ways, by virtue of their national or territorial identity: that is, by a geographical idea. But they are still *transgressive*. The fact that

ALAN RIACH

Grainger and Montgomery are Scottish opens up their position; it does not define it.

I could just as easily have taken appropriate examples from early New Zealand literature, where some poets actually wrote in the Scots language and are now considered in terms of both national traditions. If the idea of single central traditions peculiar to individual nations remains powerful, and it does, it would be, I think, strategically useful to make allies of the new literatures in English with those older literatures which share a colonial history, and Scottish literature is perhaps the most compelling of these.

More compelling at the present time, I think, than Irish literature for the very obvious reason that Irish literature is *already* considered as politically distinct. Edward Said, for example, has written eloquently on Yeats as a poet of post-colonial anti-imperialist nationalism. And it is of course no accident that James Joyce is of such vital importance to theoretical approaches to post-colonial literature. One thinks also of the splendid essay, 'Joyce and the artist's quest for a universal language' by Lloyd Fernando, which appeared in a book entitled *Cultures in Conflict: Essays on Literature and the English Language in South-East Asia* – a book published by Graham Brasch in Singapore: that is to say, at some distance from the Anglo-American critical establishment. To Fernando, what makes Joyce so relevant in South-East Asia is above all a linguistic question. If there are more than forty languages working in *Finnegans Wake*, he points out, none of them can claim total aptitude. The imperial authority of English is subsumed in the book's continuing, transformative flow. 'It is not surprising at all that before leaving Ireland the only thing [Stephen] finds himself "armed" with besides exile and cunning is – silence.'[10] Perhaps the most flagrant example of Ireland's privileged status in terms of modern literature in English is to be found in the three books on modern literature by Hugh Kenner.[11] Kenner has written one book on modern American literatue, *A Homemade World*, one on modern Irish literature, *A Colder Eye*, and one on modern 'British' literature, which bears the name *A Sinking Island*: a toilet-flush title if ever there was one. However, like so many less brilliant than himself, when Kenner says 'British' he means 'English'. His facility and wit do nothing to excuse or explain his radical neglect of political history, nor do they compensate adequately for his reluctance to engage with the political question of the British constitution. The back-cover blurb begins: 'The island, of course, is England'. But of course, there never has been an island called England.

To begin from a situation 'beyond the pale' of the Anglo-American establishment may foster a sensitivity towards interconnections that might otherwise be suppressed or excluded. Wilson Harris, who, in *Black Marsden*, has written one novel actually *set* in Scotland, fixed upon the connections between Scotland and South America with remarkable insight.[12] For Harris, the medium *and* the platform through which or by which these connections happen, is language. The most essential conquest of the rational sensibility codified in the eighteenth century by colonialism was language. Harris's English is at the furthest possible remove from the clarity of diction so much favoured by the Scottish philosophers of the Enlightenment. David Hume, purging his prose of Scotticisms, aspired to a purely English vocabulary. But the impurity, miscegenation and diversity of Harris's vision are exactly the qualities that give rise to his finely tempered sense of possibility and hope.

In the course of an interview I conducted with him in August 1990, Wilson Harris made the striking comment that in the 'Third World', what might be called 'native' archetypes 'are all overlaid by European skeletons and archetypes as well. You will never activate them unless you activate the so-called European "skeletons" as well. They are locked together and there is no way around that.'[13]

Here, I think, is the basis of a sense of language that places disparate legacies at the centre of its attention, without simplifying the ways those legacies bear on writing in *colonising* as well as colonised worlds, and the descendants of the colonised and colonizers whose inheritance they are. For Harris, new literatures are not merely branches of a host trunk growing at different speeds into mature traditions in their own right, but rather complex and rich totalities continually made up of conflicting elements in tension.

Harris provides an exemplary alternative to reductively traditionalist readings of literary history. He is a 'revisionary' writer in the best sense. What he points towards, I believe, is the possibility of reciprocal creative understanding arising from the linked dynamics of the New Literatures in English and others.

If you reject a limiting framework of 'Commonwealth' literature and, simultaneously, riddle the idea of 'English' literature with differences, you have a potentially rich (although potentially very vulnerable) area where the parameters are of less importance than the interconnections. The methodology of literary study implied by such a situation need not seek to wholly invalidate traditionalist readings – it is neither likely that it would nor desirable that it should – but it would recontextualize those traditionalist readings as much as it recontextualised the New Literatures.

If this process promotes the de-scription of Empire or the deconstruction of imperial certainties as the underlying convictions of pedagogical methodology, then all to the good.

I shall give my last word to the Scottish – or, more particularly, the Glasgow – poet Tom Leonard, the appropriateness of whose comments will not be lost in this context.[14] Leonard writes here in a phonetic imitation of urban Glasgow speech, a series of poems with a good, simple, punning title: 'Unrelated Incidents'. The Untold Stories. Except, of course, they are being truly related here:

(1)

its thi lang-
wij a thi
guhtr thaht hi
said its thi
langwij a
thi guhtr

awright fur
funny stuff
ur
Stanley Bax-
ter ur but
luv n science
n thaht naw

thi langwij
a thi
intillect hi
said thi lang-
wij a thi intill-
ects Inglish

then whin thi
doors slid
oapn hi raised
his hat geen
mi a fare-
well nod flung
oot his right

fit boldly n
fell eight
storeys
doon thi
empty
lift-shaft

(2)

ifyi stull
huvny
wurkt oot
thi diff-
rince tween
yir eyes
n
yir ears;
– geez peace,
pal!

fyi stull
huvny
thoata lang-
wij izza
sound-system;
fyi huvny
hudda thingk
aboot thi dif-
frince tween
sound
n object n
symbol; well,
ma innocent
wee
friend – iz
god said ti
adam:

a doant kerr
fyi caw it
an apple
ur
an aippl –
jist leeit
alane!

(3)

this is thi
six a clock
news thi
man said n
thi reason
a talk wia
BBC accent
iz coz yi
widny wahnt
mi ti talk
aboot thi
trooth wia
voice lik
wanna yoo
scruff. if
a toktaboot
thi trooth
lik wanna yoo
scruff yi
widay thingk
it wuz troo.
jist wanna yoo
scruff tokn.
thirza right
way ti spell
ana right way
ti tok it. this
is me tokn yir
right way a
spellin. this
is ma trooth.
yooz doant no
thi trooth
yirsellz cawz
yi canny talk
right. this is
the six a clock
nyooz. belt up.

Notes:

1 Hugh MacDiarmid, 'Preview', *Radio Times*, vol. 220, no. 2859 (26 August–1 September, 1978), p15.

2 This is a revised and expanded version of a paper delivered at the 'De-Scribing Empire Conference' held at the University of Queensland, Australia, 23–5 August 1991.

3 Bill Ashcroft, Gareth Griffiths, Helen Tiffin, *The Empire Writes Back* (London & New York: Routledge, 1989), pp. 32–3.

4 Wilson Harris, 'Unfinished Genesis: A Personal View of Crossqq Cultural Tradition', the third lecture in the Smuts Memorial Commonwealth Lectures, University of Cambridge, 7 November 1990. To be collected in Wilson Harris, *The Radical Imagination: Lectures and Talks*, ed. Alan Riach and Mark Williams.

5 I owe the formulation of this story to Mark Williams though I was present when the statement was made and I can vouch for its authenticity.

6 *The History of Scottish Literature*, vols. I–IV, general editor, Cairns Craig (Aberdeen: Aberdeen University Press, 1987–8)

7 See Peter McCarey, 'Mungo's Hat and Maxwell's Demon', *Edinburgh Review*, no. 84, 1990. And Robert Crawford, 'Ecclefechan and the Stars', *London Review of Books*, 21 January 1988.

8 Paula Burnett, ed., *The Penguin Book of Caribbean Verse in English* (Harmondsworth: Penguin Books, 1986), p. 104.

9 Ibid., p. 113.

10 Edward W. Said, *Yeats and Decolonization: A Field Day Pamphlet, no. 15* (Derry: Field Day Theatre Company Ltd, 1988). And Lloyd Fernando, 'Joyce and the Artist's Quest for a Universal Language', in *Cultures in Conflict: Essays on literature and the English language in South East Asia* (Singapore: Graham Brasob, 1986), pp. 67–82 (p. 80).

11 Hugh Kenner, *A Homemade World: The American Modernist Writers* (London: Marion Boyars, 1977), *A Colder Eye: The Modern Irish Writers* (London: Allen Lane, 1983) and *A Sinking Island: The Modern English Writers* (Baltimore: the Johns Hopkins University Press, 1989).

12 Wilson Harris, *Black Marsden (a tabula rasa comedy')* (London: Faber and Faber, 1972).

13 Wilson Harris, 'Wilson Harris interviewed by Alan Riach', to be collected in *The Radical Imagination* (see note 3).

14 Tom Leonard, 'Unrelated Incidents', in *Intimate Voices: Selected Work 1965–83* (Newcastle: Galloping Dog Press, 1984), pp. 86–94 (pp. 86–88). These are the first three poems in a sequence of seven. *Gairfish* acknowledges Tom Leonard's permission to reproduce these poems here.

GEORGE WYLLIE

Grasping a Thistle:
Scotland and the Visual Arts

On being asked for impressions of the 'avant-garde' in the visual arts in
Scotland, the thought seemed alien – it hadn't crossed my mind before.
Strangely it was the same when I mentioned it to others – the possibility
didn't seem to exist. Who then amongst us could it be – you, me, them,
that, it? The unrequired question evoked surprise at being asked, and even
after pandering, there seemed a fair expectancy that I'd deduce myself back
to square one. This does not mean that being 'avant-garde' is not within the
Scottish character – the burning thought of it is probably there, but damped
down by Calvinistic modesty.

The unpredictability of the march of new ideas makes this question a
moving target when asked anywhere. The analytical Scottish mind demands
the accurate aim of a definition and we are immediately reminded that the
'avant-garde' is a foreign phrase. The possibility of pretension by alluding
to language from elsewhere may be a turn-off to the Scot, fearing some
disguised dishonesty which makes no real difference to extending art – like
'nouvelle cuisine' does not extend food. With the question now preambled
with suspicion, I grasp the thistle and attempt a response – different from
an answer. Someone else, grasping a different thistle, would utter other
utterances, but these are mine.

Begin in Edinburgh in the sixties, and blame or praise Richard Demarco
for introducing into the Scottish art world (with the rest catching up later)
progressive artists and exhibitions from wherever. His was a virtuoso
performance which set a foundation and new standards for the extension
of art in Scotland. Scottish youth should take note of that, for at that
time visitations by the 'avant-garde' were few – and still are, but the great
exhibition 'Strategy Get Arts' with Joseph Beuys, was undoubtedly just that.
Demarco, by breaking the Victorian concept of the gallery (in particular with
his 'Journeys', which were art pilgrimages by land and sailing ship) was also
extending concepts, but the shift was not understood or approved and funding
was withdrawn, gravely upsetting his happy compass and upsetting his course
to this day. It was Beuys who set out some good ground rules which were in

tune with the Scottish character and landscape. Worlds like 'social sculpture' were bandied about. Our cool air stimulated him as it does for Scottish artists who have the soul to breath it in, for by the unavoidable primeval strength the crystal nature of this land, its thankfully small-scale urbanity, and our Celtic predilection for science, the view from the perimeter is therefore nicely balanced. In equilibrium, and free from the dazzle of elsewhere gloss, it is worth contemplating.

This clarity of air seems to nourish social and planetary conscience. It is good for art. Robert Burns's apology to a mouse and Beuys's sojourn with a coyote are attitudinally the same – just a difference of animal and emphasis. It is important not to get our cultures crossed – like Beuys locked up with a mouse or Burns addressing the coyote. Thus, the Scottish 'avant-garde' can even be unbelievably legitmate, but only when attitudes are firmly implanted in the land of Scotland. This does not preclude the use of a coyote, but only provided these terms apply – obviously Burns couldn't find one.

The great international perversity of the commercial gallery structure hardly exists here, and if a Scottish artist wishes to address that area of activity it will be more financially viable elsewhere. Thus purged, the rest of Scotland is wide open for anyone attempting to be 'avant-garde' and consequently financially precarious. There are small stretchy galleries like Glasgow's 'Transmission', Edinburgh's 'Collective' and the storm-tossed 'Demarco Gallery' – or is he rocking it himself to conjure the drift and dangers of his aborted voyage? The '369' Gallery has just spluttered to the surface after nearly gurgling to the bottom. The several University Galleries and the Art Centres in towns like Dumfries and Kilmarnock offer good opportunities. The flagship galleries, notably Edinburgh's 'Fruitmarket' and Glasgow's 'Third Eye', have recently been torpedoed but slow salvage is anticipated. The big City Galleries, especially Aberdeen and Glasgow, have occasional giddy whirls, complete with an Education Officer. Our National Gallery of Modern Art plays safe, reflecting political appointments which suggest the connoisseurial approach and the eager aspirations of merchant banking. Against this, the Society of Scottish Artists is having to fight for its annual exhibitions which, for one hundred years has had a policy of 'encouraging adventurous spirits' – which they do. Several excellent Print Studios and Sculpture Workshops are evenly spaced over the grid of Scotland, excluding no one from developing new ideas. Gaeldom is confidently represented and blessed by the most distant gallery from London I know – 'An Lanntair' ('The Lantern') in Stornoway on the Isle of Lewis, perfectly placed on the perimeter for human and planetary illumination. Mid-field is the Scottish Arts Council who believe it is their ball so we allow them to referee. Within this structure there are the usual newer forms of art, but just by being 'usual' are excluded from being 'avant-garde'. 'The British Art Show' was hosted by the Cultured European City of Glasgow in 1990, and in it there was said to be 'avant-garde' art. The heather was not set on fire, but there is always the possibility of slow combustion. Is there 'such a thing as bad 'avant-garde'? You never know with the 'avant-garde'.

With the moving target in mind, here are two significant trends instanced by two young Scottish artists in this 'British Art Show'. One, Louise Scullion, who has always been adept at making meaningful installations but usually in the safety of a gallery, and culminating in her being selected for this important exhibition. She is now artist-in-residence in a hospital in Aberdeen. I respect her tenacity of purpose and want to know how her attitude and experience will prevail in this new unsafe space. Will she be able to be 'avant garde-ish' in this new application of her art beyond the gallery? . . . The other artist is disabled and most times is in his wheelchair. There is great purpose in Brian Jenkin's work which in addition to measuring up to being substantial and meaningful on purely art terms insists that we sensibly address the honesties of relationships with the physically wounded like himself. The question is, are these activites which have germinated within the galleries now demonstrating worthwhile directions beyond the galleries? Do they stand a chance of being 'avant-garde'? Again, the artist-led 'Project Ability' protecting high-standard energy-release activities to help rectify imbalance in the community is hardly 'avant-garde' in the work it produces, but perhaps so in attitude and in the way it is applied. These artists, often unsung, are worth watching, not so much for the kudos and improvement of pedigrees, but for what they do with the dynamism of their art. But now I am justifying art by logic, and next it will be intellect, in themselves guaranteed to smother the 'avant-garde'. You can see the great danger these artists are in. 'It's not what you do but the way that you do it', sings Louis Armstrong . . . so 'Good Luck' to the unsung.

Historically art has only allowed itself to be cosseted by the gallery for a recent and short period within its evolution. Moves to social equality, heralded by the French Revolution, have enabled the ordinary citizen to emulate the affluent by regarding art mainly as art objects. This, and the institutions which support the tendency, have diverted the attitudes art is capable of stimulating by being more naturally accepted and applied within society. A saturation point for this restricted use of art is perhaps now being reached and its materialistic futility understood. But there is residual persistence to emulate the old system and all manner of covens and play-pens are invented to bolster the art pedigree, including cosmetic 'avant-garde'. There is nothing more romantic or better in type-casting as an artist – ah, the rosy wine of the artist's life! Choose from the uniformity of a carbon-dated strata of French berets, wounded corduroys, savaged jeans, and black Oxfam death suits. The outfits are harmless enough for they are only a transient confidence, but mob homage to the disguised gallery and posy-art is not, and it negates any possibility of being 'avant-garde'.

My 'Paper Boat' is now a random sister-ship to Rimbaud's 'Le Bateau Ivre'. I have sailed beyond the gallery in a confusion of ideas – mine and yours, neither being nor requiring to be called, 'avant-garde'. The description 'nouvelle cuisine' would be equally right or wrong by me. Glasgow has recently dined well on nouvelle art in nouvelle spaces, but for whatever reason has not digested the stronger meat of the visual avant-garde – a pity, for it was a Cultural City, and whilst there is no requirement to be sated, a morsel wouldn't have gone wrong – although David Mach saw to it in the 'Tramway'. In the 'Tramway', some brave new ideas in theatre – mostly from elsewhere, were well accommodated. In the streets 'TSWA3-D' events have surfaced twice in Glasgow. 'Eventspace' also allowed a group of younger artists to instal public work around the city, and recently the 'Windfall' exhibition in an adapted commercial building allowed free rein to artists from Glasgow and abroad, but almost under gallery conditions. For me, the Scottish equivalent of the 'Armory Show' was in the staid town museum in the High Street of Paisley when an energetic group from Glasgow School of Art really grabbed this bull by the balls and made a remarkable uncompromising and in every sense astonishing exhibition, the totality of which I declare, give or take, was unavoidably 'avant-garde'. It elicited public, official, art, action and reaction. The unwitting gallery suffered severe shock, and therefore I forgive the show for being indoors. The Environmental Art tutors in Glasgow's School of Art must take blame, credit, and irresponsibility for nurturing the notions of these ex-students who are still busy here and there beyond the gallery or else, alas, taking wayside computer courses.

In the continuity of art, perception of the moving target is best in retrospect. Like bathing with socks on, art relegated to the confines of the gallery is both lazy and daft. It is not that adventures cannot be demonstrated within that confine, but that it limits the audience (or vidience) which never enters the space and thus is excluded from the adventure. Most art is addressed to a safe primary audience in art schools, galleries, temporary gallery spaces and the likes. It gets cosy for the artist. This is only a broad truth – but it is absurd to deny public involvement in what is being expressed by the means chosen by artists to express it. There should be no secondary audience, only one. There is a new space for progressive sculpture in the grounds of a business park in Falkirk. The exhibitions will be changed from time to time, but the importance is that it will begin to reach a secondary audience. The work will not only test the public but will test the artists. Businessman Christos Raftopolous, in association with Glasgow School of Art and the Scottish Sculpture Trust, has funded this new concept offering the opportunity for the 'avant-garde' to go public.

Returning to the sixties and Edinburgh, another artist arrived from elsewhere, Romania, and was befriended by Demarco. He too responded to Scotland and over the years has helped sensitize the awareness that soul transcends logic and intellect. For the continuing spiral of his search for spirituality beyond ourselves, and his earth endeavours to understand the cosmic, I commend Paul Neagu as truly 'avant-garde'.

I now take a deep metaphysical breath, for the strain of this effort to identify the 'avant-garde' in Scotland is beginning to tell. With good luck and a certain amount of nurturing, the synergic condition whereby art is no longer separate from the being of a human than say, sex, pain or hunger, will make us strong and our brimful energies will solve every problem. Sure, sure, sure – and if there is perchance a surfeit of energy, then I prophesy that we will use it to think up more problems to absorb it. – Not new, but it justifies the necessity for the 'avant-garde', for if we cannot solve our problems by existing thoughts, the stark truth is that we have to get ahead of them and that's quite a trick. Everyone here knows this, and so we now understand why we Scots are reluctant to mention it for whilst inwardly admitting the frustation of having to continuously keep ahead of ourselves, we are fortunately blessed with the natural sagacity to keep the embarrassment secret, and there is dark confidence in our modesty. Is it because that Scottish analytical mind also intuitively knows the rigorous demands of the 'avant-garde', and will accept nothing less?

Ideas from brain explosions and bursts of nothing and anything – maximum minimals and minimum maximals, right-side ups and upside-inside downs are mere physical and only sometimes 'avant-garde' diversions straying from a confused deep and desperate philosophy. I now expect some response from this flexing of our unique humam capacity to reason and imagine. Being Scottish, and affected by it, there is a canny inclination not to discard any benefits this essay may deliver and to try to do something new, better – even meaningful to nurture our human and planetary conditions and spiritual sensitivity. If we should succeed by the spiral of these thoughts would it be 'avant-garde'? . . . Would it be art? . . . Would it be Scottish'? . . . Would it matter?

Meanwhile, the Planet is watching and waiting – but not for ever.

W.S. MILNE

Buchan Ness

Nor' Nor'-East we sailed,
half East fower leagues,
piling waves,
a lang cable length frae land:
wind, like suction plant
unloading grain,
a granite clock,
atween neap and spring we hauled.

Waves – strang, stane dykes, –
the gaffer
a blockhoose o a man.

Oot o Stornoway we came then
arse-end first, superstition-wise,
hame we kept in mind.
Stars were hid in pooches,
oor heids were fu o sleep.)

'For God's sake, cut the line!'
'Through the Minch we'll steer her!'
'Hadd the course! There's time!'
(Fond hope still was rinning;
hear us ower the brine.
Ti Aiberdein, Cape Wrath, the Bullers:
good anchoring left behind.)

ROBERT ALAN JAMIESON

Affinity o iddirness
To R.P.

It seems de an me ir
mistæn enannidder
fir sels 'at ir gien
t'be idder dan da wans
'at first met, yun first nicht
in Glæsgo.

Nivir leet, dønna greet:
Aa dat'll shænge quhin nixt we meet.

Fok irna free o time,
mœr as da tides ir,
or gæls it come by,
in sæsin, shæstin time oot,
trowe da door, trowe da grind
ahint wis.

Nivir leet, dønna greet:
Aa dat'll shænge quhin da møn's gien in.

Da dæk atween 'is, isna big
bit's dær aa da sam.
Lat's shak haands, across
da stonn, move on da sam,
de dy wye, me my wye,
back ida rig.

Nivir leet, dønna greet:
dy rig micht be iddir, bit da ært's wir's bæth.

TOM HUBBARD

Doktor Faust ti Doktor Jekyll

Oor daurkest leir has left us unacquent
Wi the flaucht that chairges bairns an luvers an makars,
That kythes in an instant the innermaist lilt o leevin,
Whan seein an hearin wi taste an touch are as ane:
Ay, thaim an mair. Fir us, thae quair o oors,
That Lang an lane we sweitit ti unsneck,
Nae suner we're ben and blythe – but they snack shut,
An aa the brees that trauchled throu oor bodies
gar broun-edged pages turn but anerlie brouner,
Wi us the flettened flouers – gin you'd cry us flouers –
That hinna lately blumed as aince we blumed
Ayont the festinance o foustie chaumers.

My fallow Doktor and my fallow Harry,
Fallow in muckle else, we differ in this,
That whaur I'd nou conneck, you wad cut aff;
That whaur I'd be mair tentie, you wad ignore;
That whaur I'd maister Mephistopheles
Afore he maisters me, you creesh his loof,
Tell him ti nab whitever he wants o you,
Gin he'd anerlie leave you snod as an Embro elder.

O Harry, it's nae bi rivin spreit frae corpus,
Harn frae hert, or even guid fae ill:
It's whether we chuse ti tak the pairt or the hale:
You hae taen the pairt; the lave sall venge itsel.
Your frien, your Faust, has lairnt this weill an sair
That's thon a skeelie serpens maks retour
Aye wormin throu your waa, your desk, your buik:
I'd brust the door, walcome the bruit inside
Ti gar him kythe himsel. You bid him . . . *Hyde*.

Leir – learning; flaucht – flame, excitement; kythes – reveals;
quairs – books; lane – lone; sweitit ti unsneck – sweated to unlock;
ben an blythe – inside and happy; snack – snap; brees – juices;
anerlie – only; hinna – have not; festinance-confinement; foustie
chaumirs – musty chambers; fallow – fellow; conneck – connect;
tentie – watchful; creesh his loof – grease his palm; snod – neat, comfortable; Embro – Edinburgh; spreit – spirit; harn – brain; hert –
heart; hale – whole; lave – rest; venge – avenge; skeelies serpens –
skilful serpent; retour – return.

The Daith o Faust

(Free transcreatioun, fae the German
o the Italo-German music-makar, Ferruccio
Busoni)

Bairn, I lay you here:
I scrieve the circle roun you.
I will my life ti you:
Lat it growe
Fae the yird-fest ruits
o my dwtynin-time
Ti the bud an the blume
o your becomin.
Sae I weave on in you,
As you sall weave in turn,
An dell deeper an deeper
The merk o my bein.

Whaur I misbiggit,
Mak you remeid;
Whit I negleckit
Tak ti its heid.
Sae I sall win
Abune the laws
Formin as ane
The three pairts o time,
An mellin mysel
Wi aa the unborn . . .

Yird – earth; dwynin – dwindling; bein – being; misbiggit – built
badly; remeid – remedy; mellin – mingling, blending.

PSEUDORCA

The Word Tax

The failure of the Word Tax in Scotland has proven a most salutary lesson to the British government. Critics of the system had warned ministers that the basic assumption behind the tax – that we all spoke the same language – was not strictly tenable. But few could have foreseen just how awry this supposedly foolproof plan for increasing revenue would go. How naive early slogans now seem: 'Put your money where your mouth is.' 'Look after the syllables, and the sentences will look after themselves!'

A predictable response soon appeared in spraypaint on the sides of Glasgow's subway trains and the housing estates of Dundee: 'A penny for your thoughts? Say no more!' And the first opponents of the Word Tax were indeed those who refused to say anything at all. These divided into two main groups, the Mime Artists of Caledonia, and the Grand Order of Amateur Trappists. The first of these sects believed that no reference should be made to speech at all, whilst the other permitted its members to carry round single words to show to shopkeepers and others. Attempts to amalgamate into a mass movement called the Silent Majority broke up over these points of dogma, and the two cults are still not speaking to each other.

But the principle impediment to the tax's enforcement turned out to be one of interpretation. Recording the numbers of words used in Scotland, then gradating them according to the numbers of syllables employed, might seem an insurmountable problem in itself. However the growth of the native electronics industry, as well as the readiness of a significant minority of the population with taperecorders, notepads, and even the backs of envelopes, proved more than adequate to this challenge. The real difficulty only arose when government officials attempted to evaluate the raw materials thus assembled.

The use of computers to facilitate the process came to nothing as a result of the so-called 'Shropshire effect'. This is the failure of any present spell-check programme to cope with the variety of human speech; thus the word 'Shropshire' is corrected to 'shoplifter'. Attempts to amend this problem made nonsense of a large number of police files, particularly as the term 'sent to Shropshire' rapidly acquired a criminal meaning in relation to stolen goods.

The democratic deployment of equal numbers of English and Scots civil servants also turned out to be counter-productive. Serious disagreements broke out over the meanings of perfectly ordinary terms. The word 'messages' was taken by some to be 'of specialised use, relating to communication; possibly financial, possibly with foreign or supernatural agents'. Others felt it to be 'of domestic origin, relating to the purchase of comestibles, hardware, and other necessary items.' The word 'supper' was also found to be problematic; some officials felt it signified 'a romantic tryst, possibly relating to cohabitation,' whilst others insisted it meant 'junk food featuring chipped potatoes'.

Then there was the response of nationalist intransigents and other less innocuous elements. Faced with a perfectly fair tax on plain standard English, these retreated into an incomprehensible thicket of dialect. Words such as 'hullawrerr' or 'hoozitgaun', subject to tax as 'three syllable terms, possibly of technical origin', were claimed by these types to be a series of separable monosyllables with the occasional dissyllable thrown in, and therefore taxable at the lower rate. Legal disputes of this nature soon choked the courts.

A partial solution was achieved by consulting linguistic experts, who established that a number of these verbal extremists were employing obsolete words or words with a purely literary usage. Attempts to tax such terms at a higher rate exacerbated both Scottish conservatives and English liberals, who claimed this constituted an attack on Scottish culture. Ministers, ordinarily proof to such paranoid assertions, were forced to back down in the face of mounting public outcry. This created the infamous 'Backspang', or 'Vernacular loophole'.

The most outrageous neologisms spread, as the people turned to their poets and lexicographers for inspiration. All such terms fell into the 'protected' bracket as long as they appeared in 'literature' or the pseudo-dictionaries published in such numbers at this period. Thus words like 'motor car', 'nuclear power plant' or 'smoked salmon', all previously taxable as luxury items, fell within the orbit of working class speakers when they became 'thi sharabangir', 'English flu' and 'smeekie' (as in the phrase 'Eh'll hae a smeekie suppir but mak ut fast coz thi sharabangir's oan a doobil yella – an nane o thae wans wi English flu!').

A prolonged smear campaign was launched by prominent Anglo-Scots, and television critics ridiculed popular programmes in which national heroes like Rab C. Nesbit vigorously espoused the new jargon. Defeat was acknowledged, however, when a character on 'The Fresh Prince of Bel Air' was heard to enquire 'Well help ma boab wass happnin dude?'

The upsurge in nationalist feeling had reached such a pitch that the British government felt only one response was left: they held a referendum. Counting on the legendary inability of the Scots to agree about anything amongst themselves, they went to the country. A sample batch of 'representative' words was selected, and the people were asked to indicate their support (or lack of it) for government-sponsored definitions. On the basis of these findings, it was argued, a new system of absolute meaning would be established.

The definitions

1. Gaelic

    a) Something to do with France.
    b) A smelly vegetable that has something to do with France.
    c) The language of some of the Highlands and Islands of Scotland.

2. Scotch

    a) A drink to have with soda or shortbread, depending on country of imbibation.
    b) People from Scotland or their things.
    c) To burn, slash, destroy and otherwise extirpate.

3. English

    a) A form of radiation that mutates the brain into a terrified mollusc unable to master a constantly shifting series of useless social rules.
    b) Us.
    c) What you speak when not indulging in cat-and-mouse tactics in which you are – let's face it – the mouse.

4. Democracy

    a) The system whereby a bunch of idiots are ruled by people only marginally more in grasp of the situation.
    b) The system whereby all are equal and have a say in the system.
    c) Anything we need it to be.

5. Money

    a) The true, original and unalterable language of these islands and anywhere else in the universe for that matter.
    b) What we've got lots more of.
    c) What you'd better continue to want.

Not surprisingly a number of Scots spoilt their ballot sheets by scribbling a fourth and sometimes a fifth definition on the bottom. One person, a self-proclaimed 'bard', inscribed ten further definitions on the back in a minute and clearly obsessive hand, then asked for several loose sheets of A4 to be taken into consideration. This would have been enough in itself had not a sizeable number also signed a petition stating that they no longer accepted any definition whatsoever of any of the terms included on the voting slip. Furthermore they declared that they would no longer employ any such terms or any objects associated with them (with the exceptions of 1, categories (b) *and* (c), and 2, category (a)).

This clinched the matter. Not only were the Scots dangerous anarchists, they were dangerous inconsistent anarchists. Permission was given for wealthy refugees from Hong Kong to create a 'fifth city' on the newly-vacated Holy Loch. A number of 'neo-crannogs' were made available by using the split hulls of scrapped British submarines (and incidentally showing these poet Johnnies weren't the only ones able to make up a word or two). Chinese was declared the national language of Scotland, and development grants were only made available to those who spoke it. The province was renamed 'New Northern Ireland'. Sectarian unrest grew to the point where troops had to be sent in, and, with a tank on every street corner, the obstreperous little voice of the Scots soon found it had something new to shout about.

SECOND CITIES
by Donny O'Rourke

Glasgow Herald Critic's Choice 1991

£4.99   ISBN 0951695908   32pp

VENNEL PRESS
9 Pankhurst Court, Caradon Close, London, E11 4TB